Analysing Media Discourses

Edited by
John E. Richardson and
Joseph D. Burridge

Routledge
Taylor & Francis Group

LONDON AND NEW YORK

First published 2011
by Routledge
2 Park Square, Milton Park, Abingdon, Oxon, OX14 4RN

Simultaneously published in the USA and Canada
by Routledge
711 Third Avenue, New York, NY 10017

Routledge is an imprint of the Taylor & Francis Group, an informa business

First issued in paperback 2012

This book is a reproduction of *Social Semiotics* 18.3. The Publisher requests that those citing this book use the bibliographical details of the journal issue on which the book is based.

Typeset in Times New Roman by Taylor & Francis Books.

British Library Cataloguing in Publication Data
A catalogue record for this book is available from the British Library

ISBN13: 978-0-415-61858-8 (hbk)
ISBN13: 978-0-415-63224-9 (pbk)

Disclaimer

The publisher would like to make readers aware that the chapters in this book are referred to as articles as they had been in the special issue. The publisher accepts responsibility for any inconsistencies that may have arisen in the course of preparing this volume for print.

Contents

Notes on Contributors

John E. Richardson: Newcastle University, Newcastle, UK.

Joseph D. Burridge: University of Portsmouth, Portsmouth, UK.

Alex Wade: Independent Scholar, UK.

Elizabeth Stokoe: Loughborough University, Loughborough, UK.

Jim McGuigan: Loughborough University, Loughborough, UK.

Scott Cherry: Independent Scholar, UK.

Jane Liffen: Independent Scholar, UK.

Michael Pickering: Loughborough University, Loughborough, UK.

Georgina Turner: Independent Scholar, UK.

INTRODUCTION

Recent years have seen a growth in mass-mediated cultural artefacts and a concomitant growth in their social and cultural significance. Academia has been relatively quick to respond to some of these apparent changes (see, for example, Deacon et al. 2007; Talbot 2007; Matheson 2005). This has resulted in an expansion of analytic approaches (cf. Barnhurst and Nerone 2001; Bell and Garrett 1998; Cotter 1996; Fairclough 1995; Kress and van Leeuwen 2006; Machin 2007; Martin and White 2005; McGuigan 1997; Pickering 2008; Richardson 2007; Titscher et al. 2000) to make sense of the semiotic processes involved in contemporary mass communications, their relations to wider social and structural systems (for instance, markets, political formations, the law), as well as the consequences they may have on textual, discursive and social practices.

A degree of reflection upon the range of approaches available for making sense of contemporary and historical media discourse is appropriate and desirable, and this timely special issue showcases a broad range of existing techniques for analysing various mass-mediated texts. These include newspapers, magazines (contemporary editorial content, and historical advertising), books (covers and contents, and in two genres), party political leaflets, television programmes (situation comedy, and so-called "reality" television), and computer games. In examining these varied media, the contributors to this special issue have drawn upon an equally varied range of methods and approaches to the analysis of texts and discourse. These include, among others, critical discourse analysis, conversation analysis, ethnomethodology, cultural studies, psychoanalysis, rhetorical and ideological analysis, multi-modal methods, and social theory.

The majority of papers in this special issue are highly empirical in focus, and those that are less so provide rich and important theoretical insights. Each of these articles represents the use of a methodology without guarantees, and – it is important to stress – without any *essential* relationship to the material they analyse. Nevertheless, they produce robust analytical insights that illuminate important aspects of the ways in which contemporary, and historical, meaning-making works, and show approaches to working with mediated material "in action" – illustrating, among other things, how to analyse media texts of various types.

Firstly, in the most theoretically-driven piece in the issue, Alex Wade explores ways of conceptualising how different types of space interrelate with one another, drawing upon and developing the work of Lefebvre. He emphasises the fluidity of contemporary social life, as well as wider social and technological changes, and advances the conception of "trans-space" to account for the way that contemporary mediation leads to a situation in which multiple spaces can be, and are, inhabited at once. This conception is explained through a series of fictional illustrations, before being applied and exemplified as part of an "ethnographic sketch" of the operation and use of an amateur flight simulator. Wade shows how this highly sophisticated computer program allows, and requires, the simultaneously habitation of different types of space, as well as identifying how this operates, and the impact that this can have upon the users in a practical context.

In her article, Elizabeth Stokoe utilises conversation analytic understandings of social interaction to show how television script-writers apply their mundane practical knowledge about the organisation of talk in order to generate humour for an audience. Specifically, she demonstrates how the script of American situation comedy *Friends* utilises breaches of normative conversational organisation in this regard. Rather than relying upon "joke-telling", she demonstrates how the juxtaposition of normatively "appropriate" and "inappropriate" turns in conversational sequences can function to produce laughter. Her emphasis is therefore upon the ways in which mundane features of talk – adjacency pairs such as questions and answers, invitations and acceptances (or declinations), apologies and acceptances (or declinations) – can be used humorously. Specifically, Stokoe's analysis shows the interdependence between the application of mundane knowledge in the design of the script and its humour and the audience's assumed mundane knowledge of normative conversational practices, and therefore the extent to which these semiotic and pragmatic repertoires are assumed to be widely shared by writers and audiences alike. By utilising screenshots from the programme, her paper is also able to identify the synergy between linguistic discourse and image, in a manner also present in contributions from Burridge, Liffen, Pickering, and Richardson.

Taking an altogether more directly critical, but less micro-analytical, approach to a television programme, Jim McGuigan offers a cultural studies reading of the British and American editions of the "reality" television programme *The Apprentice*. McGuigan examines the franchise as an example of "Cool Capitalism" – a contemporary cultural tendency in which signs of rebellion, disaffection and resistance are incorporated into the products of capitalism to construct it, capitalism, as "cool". In this sense, he argues, *The Apprentice* is educative, teaching the "serious fun" of capitalist production through the genre of sporting entertainment. In his examination, McGuigan detects several ideological tensions that run throughout the programme, notably in the collaboration that is required between "contestants" in order to win the competition, and the ways that signs of "coolness" and rebellion are reclaimed in the name of conformist commercialism. He concludes by arguing that while it is self-evident the programme projects the values of free-market business, it does this whilst "appealing to people, in a sense, on their own ground" – through embedding them in a soap-operatic game show, attuned to the national milieu in which it is produced and consumed.

The next cultural artefact to receive attention is the "self-help" book, and Scott Cherry utilises ethnomethodological insights to explore it in some detail. He focuses in particular on an apparent paradox at the heart of the self-help genre: that such books are simultaneously portrayed as self-contained media for the pursuit of self-help, while, at the same time, they tend to portray the reading of the book itself as insufficient for self-help to be successfully achieved. Cherry shows how the self-help book constructs its reader as both the location of a problem and the solution to his/her circumstances, with their transition from one state to the other being mediated by their reading of the self-help book. However, self-help really does not take place until *extra-textual* practices are implemented *subsequent* to this process of reading. There is a prioritisation of *doing* over and above the activity of *reading*, such that the reader of the book is rhetorically constructed as the accountable agent for activities that must take place beyond the process of reading.

Books are also the medium analysed by Jane Liffen in her article, although the focus here is on their covers. She examines the cover of two romance novels depicting Scottish female herring workers and the relationship of these images to the contents of the books. The extent to which these visual representations can be seen as conforming to, or subverting, the genre of romantic fiction is explored, as well as their portrayal of the working realities of female herring labour, as understood from both historical accounts and testimonies she collected in oral history interviews. Liffen discusses the portrayal of gender in the two covers, and the plot contents, as well as identifying some of the highly symbolic reasons for excluding certain features of herring work from the front-cover illustrations. Although part of the everyday reality of the lives of herring workers, knives and blood – by being "abject" – are symbolic elements likely to be subversive of the romance genre in various ways.

In his contribution, John Richardson applies critical discourse analytic and multi-modal methods to a pair of local election leaflets distributed by the British National Party and Labour Party in Bradford in 2006. He explores their respective constructions of race and nation, and identifies ways in which the prejudiced discourse of the extreme Right is incorporated into more mainstream political discourse, and is thereby allowed to influence the agenda on certain issues – specifically that of immigration. In particular, Richardson identifies an orientation towards English exceptionalism in the leaflets of both Labour and the British National Party, along with a construction of migrants as objects to be managed in "Our" interests. While the British National Party leaflet engages in a range of discursive practices to construct Islam as a threat, the Labour leaflet constructs a version of English tolerance as facilitating a multi-cultural nation in which managed migration of the ethnic Other is welcome because of its economic benefits to "Us". This construction of a united nation occurs, in part, through an associated elision of class and other differences.

Georgina Turner also uses critical discourse analysis in her article, examining *Diva*, the UK's only mainstream – that is, mass-distributed – lesbian magazine. As she points out, despite the sizeable literature examining the form and functions of magazines aimed at and consumed by heterosexual women, work analysing in-group media representations of lesbians is far more limited. Taking six editions of the magazine (August 2002–January 2003), Turner focuses on the ways that the writers and editors of the magazine attempt to construct and regulate a sense of in-group identity through editorial texts. Her analysis is presented in two sections: the first addressing the construction of "the lesbian community", and the second examining how "they" – those outside this community – are constructed, including the tensions that *Diva* constructs between these groups. In discussing this constructed binary, Turner pays attention to the complex and unstable position of bisexual women and gay men, as "border groups" and part-time allies, and the ways that they, too, are frequently positioned as part of "Them" according to what she terms a "queer ideological square".

A critical approach to discourse is also taken by Michael Pickering, in exploring the recurring use of racial stereotypes in tabloid news. Pickering takes a front-page tabloid news story to examine how the social and symbolic categories used in news reporting often draw on and reproduce stereotypical ideas developed in previous historical formations. The story itself – from *The Sun*, Monday 7 February 1994 – concerned adultery and the abandonment of a husband and family by a middle-aged white British woman who fell in love with a young black man while on holiday in Gambia. Pickering shows how the narrative of the report privileges certain "voices" and silences others, and plays on the fear and fascination of the sexualised "racial Other". Moreover, in intertextual concert with an accompanying front-page article, the report draws upon age-old racist notions of "Our" civilisation and "Their" primitiveness.

In his article, Joseph Burridge examines a corpus of food adverts published in British women's magazines while rationing was in place in Britain – during and immediately following the Second World War. He argues, first, that two competing narratives summing up advertising during this period of history, which categorise adverts as either frugality-orientated or consumption-orientated, are unduly simplistic and therefore insufficient in grasping the form and function of these texts. A more useful approach, he argues, is one that attends to the ways that advertising during this period rhetorically managed the scarcity of items *at the same time* as advocating their consumption. It is such an approach that directs his article, drawing on the concept of the "ideological dilemma" from Billig et al. (1988). Focusing in particular on adverts for products explicitly identified as unavailable, his examination demonstrates how the tensions between apparently opposing social systems and activities – such as ideologies of frugality and consumption – can be used as a *rhetorical resource* by advertisers, in various ways.

Together, these articles indicate some of the breadth of contemporary approaches to analysing media discourses as well as some of the overlaps and interconnections between studies in this area. Of course, the selected articles, and the issue as a whole, are not offered as a comprehensive inventory of the methods available to contemporary media analysts – conspicuously absent, for example, are the ethnographic methods that have done so much to illuminate the practices of media production (Cotter 1996; Machin 2002; Machin and Niblock 2004; van Hout and Jacobs 2008). However, although necessarily selective, we hope that, collectively, readers find this special issue interesting and useful, and that it contributes to the continuing maturation of media discourse studies. It only remains for us to thank the editorial collective – particularly Terry, Paul and David – for their advice, encouragement and enthusiasm throughout the development of this special issue, the contributing authors for their work and the reviewers for their supportive criticism of the articles.

References

Barnhurst K.G., and J. Nerone. 2001. *The form of news: A history.* New York: Guilford Press.

Bell, A., and P. Garrett, eds. 1998. *Approaches to media discourse.* Oxford: Blackwell.

Billig, M., S. Condor, D. Edwards, M. Gane, D. Middleton, and A. Radley. 1988. *Ideological dilemmas: A social psychology of everyday thinking.* London: Sage.

Cotter, C. 1996. Irish on the air: Media, discourse, and minority-language development. Unpublished PhD diss., University of California, Berkeley.

Deacon, D., M. Pickering, P. Golding, and G. Murdock. 2007. *Researching communications.* London: Hodder Arnold.

Fairclough, N. 1995. *Media discourse.* London: Arnold.

Kress, G., and T. van Leeuwen. 2006. *Reading images: The grammar of visual design.* London: Routledge.

Machin, D. 2002. *Ethnographic research for media students.* London: Hodder Arnold.

———. 2007. *Introduction to multimodal analysis.* London: Hodder Arnold.

Machin, D., and S. Niblock. 2004. *News production.* London: Routledge.

Martin, J.R., and P.R.R. White. 2005. *The language of evaluation: Appraisal in English.* London and New York: Palgrave/Macmillan.

Matheson, D. 2005. *Media discourses.* Maidenhead: Open University Press.

McGuigan, J. 1997. *Cultural methodologies.* London: Sage.

Pickering, M., ed. 2008. *Research methods for cultural studies.* Edinburgh: Edinburgh University Press.

Richardson, J.E. 2007. *Analysing newspapers: An approach from critical discourse analysis.* Houndmills: Palgrave.

Talbot, M. 2007. *Media discourse: Representation and interaction.* Edinburgh: Edinburgh University Press.

Titscher, S., M. Meyer, R. Wodak, and E. Vetter. 2000. *Methods of text and discourse analysis: In search of meaning.* London: Sage.

Van Hout, T., and G. Jacobs. 2008. News production theory and practice: Fieldwork notes on power, interaction and agency. *Pragmatics* 18, no. 1: 59–86.

John E. Richardson and Joseph D. Burridge

Space pilot: an introduction to amateur flight simulation

Alex Wade

Life in twenty-first-century societies is complex, interdependent and changeable. Taking this consideration as its starting point, this article examines how spatial analysis comprehends this fluidity. With the theoretical emphasis on Henri Lefebvre, I look to examine how the classic triadic model of lived, conceived and perceived space can be updated to include those areas of space whereby society is in a state of flux, manifested by the apparently indiscernible switches between a variety of spaces. The constant movement and habitation of a multitude of spaces, I call "trans-space". Expanding upon this, the article argues that a revision of Lefebvre's typology should include "digital" and "enchanted" space to allow for a more nuanced comprehension of how space interrelates. This model is then applied to the ethnographic study of an amateur flight simulator, showing how individuals transfer between spaces, how spaces act when they are brought together and how they simultaneously complement and resist one another.

Introduction

The central conceit of life in the twenty-first century is of a complex, interdependent world. Life is lived as augmented and abetted by an array of technologies, used to communicate with people, and, increasingly with themselves. Living space is squeezed into urban centres as the global population increases and émigrés look to post-industrial societies for work that the native population cannot or will not undertake, while the native populace looks for solace elsewhere: a holiday here, a house in the country there, contributing to a vast throughput of flows of people, goods, information, endlessly circulating, constricted only by individual perceptions of time, space and money.

This is not without precedent. Over a decade ago Castells wrote of the "space of flows", which are "the programmable sequences of exchange and interaction between physically disjointed positions" (Castells 1996, 442). Developing this, Mol and Law regard these spaces as "variation without boundaries, and transformation without discontinuity ... The space we are dealing with is fluid" (Mol and Law cited in Urry 2000, 31), and becomes a key part in the formation of Urry's thesis of a sociology of mobilities that makes "instantaneous time and new kinds of space central to how social life is configured" (Urry 2000, 190). This new kind of space is illustrated by the metaphor of the "semi-privatised capsule" of the automobile trailblazing the routes we voyage through life, using the car as an extension of the self and mediation with the fantasia of non-places where the "human being is immersed within the technology and vice versa" (Urry 2000, 192). Perhaps, in hindsight, it would be best to see mobile societies as best served by the trope of the mobile phone – as shown by de Souza's study of *keitai* (portable phones) culture in Japan, where users spend inordinate amounts of time waiting for and travelling on rapid transport systems and so use phones for communication, Internet surfing and gaming, resulting in "hybrid spaces" where "one no longer needs to go out of physical space to get in touch with digital environments" (de Souza 2006, 264). The mixing of spaces is also evidenced at airport terminals, which show an "incorporation of digital and media spaces" (Lloyd 2003, 104), with the widespread use of Internet kiosks and "real-time" flight updates creating "a kind of hyperspace ... with the erasure of spaces in between" (Lloyd 2003, 106). The worlds of high-speed travel of minimal resistance are mediated with signs of prescription, instruction and prohibition finding their ultimate signifier in Augé's "non-places", which, "unlike Baudelarian modernity, do not integrate the earlier places" (Augé 1995, 78).

The theme emerging from the literature is best seen as a dissolving of the boundaries of how space is notionally understood. Transition from the non-place of the airport or service station to the digital/conceived space of the Global Positioning System (GPS) cannot be easily delineated. Furthermore, the attribution of post-humanism to everyday life and the impact of cybernetics – as evinced by Haraway (1991), Hayles (1999) and embodied by Stelarc – has not, it would seem, come to pass (see Muri 2003). The conceptual inspiration for these works, Gibson's "cyberspace" and Stephenson's "metaverse", more closely resemble the Internet and *Second Life* (Linden Lab 2003) respectively, both of which require a physical body that is separate from the digital, even if technological extensions of the body (a mouse, a joypad, a handset) are required to properly access them. These extensions of humanity into different media and spaces are well documented in McLuhan (2006/1964) but also have close identification with Merleau-Ponty, who identifies a "motor space opening up beneath my hands, in which I am about to 'play' what I have read" (Merleau-Ponty 1962/1945, 144) when using his typewriter. Crucially, Merleau-Ponty – like McLuhan and Urry after him – identifies the communication between technology and humanity as a two-way process, with space as the interface.

With the examination of space and technology at the fore, accompanied by the conceptual development of Henri Lefebvre's key works, the present article will attempt to construct a typology of contemporary spaces, and promote an analysis of how individuals and groups occupy two or more spaces at one time. The means for this mediation and transition I call *trans-space*. Trans-space shows how the flux of contemporary life can be examined and how corollary and contradictory spaces can be incorporated into a coherent entity. To demonstrate this, the article will present instances of how different spaces (e.g. digital, enchanted, perceived) are navigated and traversed, before offering an ethnographic investigation of trans-spaces in regards to a flight simulator, part of my current topic of research into videogames.

Lefebvre

Lefebvre's model is highly influential in the study of geographies of space (Soja 1996) and the social theory it lends itself to (Elden 2004; Shields 1999). Soja proclaims Lefebvre's approach to be "transdisciplinary" (Soja 1996, 6) and this protean quality is often reflected in his work. His opus *The Production of Space* (Lefebvre 1991) notes the importance of transition within both spaces, "medium sized squares and streets which are the transitional and connecting spaces" (Lefebvre 1991, 154–155), and objects, "a window ... [a]s a transitional object has two senses, two orientations: from inside to outside and from outside to inside" (Lefebvre 1991, 209) to the constitution of society. However, the transitional realm is viewed as just that: a means by which his primary model of perceived space, conceptualised space and lived space (Lefebvre 1991, 38–39) can be accessed. Following Lefebvre, it is helpful to understand the spatial triad through consideration of the body:

(1) *Perceived Space* – how the body uses its senses of perception to comprehend and interpret the space it is in. For example, a piece of grass may be seen as an area of recreation for children, but an hour's work for the gardener.

(2) *Conceived Space* – the body as an arena for scientific knowledge, especially pertinent with the ideological migration from research on the physical world (astronomy) to the biological world (genetic and cybernetic augmentation).

(3) *Lived Space* – the body as a parchment that both reads and instructs the world around it. A bedroom is a quintessential lived space as ritual, romance and recuperation combine to provide a private area of bodily retreat that is both symbolic and practical. (Adapted from Lefebvre 1991, 40)

In common with Merleau-Ponty and other existentialists, Lefebvre viewed the concrete application of his model as crucial to understanding his thought lest it amount to "no more than that of one ideological mediation among others" (Lefebvre 1991, 40). Unfortunately, he also shares Merleau-Ponty's penchant for abstruse writing. His aim with the triadic model, however, is clear: that "the individual may move from one [space] to another without confusion" (Lefebvre 1991, 40). At this point it is useful to figuratively illustrate the interconnection of the lived, perceived and conceived realms as would be comprehended by Lefebvre when writing his treatise in the early 1970s. Following Lefebvre's intimation (1991, 294–295), I am using the Venn diagram to best formulate this (Figure 1).

Taking the top circle as representative of lived space, the left circle as perceived space, and the right circle as conceived space, interconnectedness and the ability to fluidly move from one space to another can be seen as a key component of Lefebvre's archetype. Additionally, it allows for pure spaces to be inhabited by an individual. For example, a person asleep in their bed would be in a purely lived space and would be at the zenith of the lived space circle; a child kicking a can and pretending to be a famous footballer is in a purely perceived, fictional space and resides on the far left of the perceptual circle; a patient involved in a surgical operation inhabits a purely conceived space of science and is therefore on the far right of the conceived circle. Central to this discussion of trans-space is the idea that many spaces can be inhabited simultaneously. To enable clearer under-standing, imagine meeting Alison Sims, a fictional female student who provides a concrete, relational example of trans-space and its related typology. Alison has finished classes for the day and is walking down the street. She perceives those around her; assimilates and

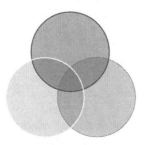

Figure 1.   Venn diagram showing interconnections between space.

disseminates the rules, rituals and symbols of lived space (crossing at the zebra crossing, thanking the driver); and concurrently absorbs the conceptual spaces of billboard and shop-window advertising, offering an abstract future of ideal body-types and non-places of possible travel destinations. Alison would find herself in the middle of Lefebvre's diagrammatic representation, with the dominant spatial influence oscillating depending on gaze, state of mind, interaction, experience and motivation. This state of flux is the process of trans-space, the rapid and fluid movement between different types of space, often without one being aware of the fluctuation. Fluid, transitive and hectic, it offers an appropriate diagnostic of the nexus of life in twenty-first-century post-industrial societies.

Trans-space

This seemingly interminable immersion in trans-space, characterised by 24-hour broad-casting and retail, Internet and mobile phone use – often simultaneously – is alluded to by Lefebvre's model but does not adequately accommodate the complexities and subtleties of daily life for the inhabitant of the contemporary world. Consider Alison once again. Before she enters her purely lived space of the bedroom, she prepares herself for sleep through ritual and habit, brushing her teeth, washing herself, drawing the curtains. Part of these lived-space rituals may be perceived – she feels more weary as she climbs into bed; some may be conceived – setting the alarm clock to provide a conception of time that will eventually become both perceived (it is time to get up) and lived (the reversed ritual of going to bed). So far, so standard. However, as Alison falls into deep sleep she begins to dream. She remains in the distinctly lived space of the bed, yet she views herself as being somewhere different; on holiday with her boyfriend, swimming in a redolent sea. It can be argued that she is in a perceived space, yet perception requires sensory apparatus to discern the relationships between spaces and objects, although she may be active in perceiving and interpreting the dream at a later time. Furthermore, her dream cannot be perceived by others, and is rarely understood *in toto* by the incumbent or the conceived spaces of medical professionals. Following this, the space that Alison occupies I call "enchanted". Within the typology of trans-space, enchanted space has fluid, interconnected relations with lived and perceived space, and is the secluded space of the inexplicable and/or intimate. Sociology, as a "science", has an uneasy relationship with the enigmatic, yet there remain arenas that even the most focused of conceived spaces cannot explain, but are clearly evident in everyday life (Broks 2004), even if these become, over time, homologised into science.

The following day, Alison gets up and, after reflecting on her dream while eating breakfast, sits in front of her PC and accesses the Internet. The action of sitting down, turning on the computer, and accessing the Internet is suggestive of two types of space. Firstly, there is ritualisation, a bodily transition from one form of interaction with the world, the directly lived space of her room, to another, one that Lefebvre would view as a conceived space. Secondly, there is a performative transition, whereby the computer enters a transitional space of booting up *Windows*, before both Alison and the computer jointly go through the Internet *portal*, resulting in a screen where a *home* page is proffered. At this point in space, Ms Sims is part of a grid of millions of other users, yet she is both at home in the performative sense of the Internet home page and in the sense of her inhabiting a lived space. Additionally, she perceives the information of the screen, which may contain conceived spaces of advertising. The negative impingement of the conceived space of information technology onto lived space and everyday life is well documented (Baudrillard 1988, 16) and prompted Lefebvre to ask as early as 1981: "[will] computer science with its repercussions and related disciplines go as far to transform everyday life?" (Lefebvre 2006, 136). The answer is an unequivocal yes. The possibilities available to Alison in accessing this space are myriad. She can communicate with arenas of work (library catalogues), consumption (Internet shopping) and leisure (gaming), and interact with others (email). This is the space of the "digital". Separate, but nevertheless interlinked to conceived, perceived and lived spaces, the digital is a venue that allows for the projection of the self over distance in a short period of time. The Internet is the current paradigm of digital space, merging diffuse aspects of life into one, generally static, often lived space (although this is altering as wireless area networks permeate urban space) location. The physical spatial distancing of the individual from subject and object is called "telæsthesia", allowing for perception at a distance. Conceptually and etymologically, this is found in all technologies that enable the paradoxical yet synchronised projection and distancing of the self as shown by the telegraph, telephone, television and telecommunications (Wark 2007, 55). It is also interesting to note that the path taken by this method of innovation has culminated in the science of "telematics", where integration of information technology with telecommunications is paramount, and not, as some have previously suggested, the fusion of human and machine.

Therefore, trans-space is not merely the action of movement between spaces, but also the status of inhabiting multiple spaces at any given time. As the above discussion demonstrates, in post-industrial societies this is the most common site of spatial residence, with everyday life seen as a series of instantaneous, invisible switches between different spaces. Furthermore, it is important to remember that "digital" and "enchanted" spaces do not replace or supersede any aspect of Lefebvre's conceptual triad, but augment it. Although it is conceptually possible – as late twentieth-century cyberpunk literature envisions – for an individual or community to fully inhabit digital and enchanted space, this is unlikely to occur due to limitations of the body and perception of/by the self, preventing exclusive absorption. Concurrently, if perceived, conceived and lived spaces are the nature of spatial analysis, then digital and enchanted spaces are what is nurtured by them. In this respect they can come to be viewed as the *culture*, which is produced by the dominant spatial terms. It is no coincidence that there is a correlating increase in the digital and the enchanted (Davis 2004). This can be seen in the analogous proliferation of laptops and self-help books, mobile phones and spiritual bookshops. It is worthy of further consideration that when Alison embarks on a train journey, she takes the lived, perceived, enchanted space of the book with her (seen as a withdrawal from her immediate surroundings) and the conceived, perceived, digital space of her mobile phone (seen as a distancing and projection), and may access both at the same time. While Alison has *learnt* how to read, she *uses* the phone; where one involves interpretation, the other is a technical process. In essence, one provides meaning (means-orientated) and the other utility (ends-orientated), but these distinctions are not always clear; the conflation of the mystery (as incomprehension) of technology and the mysticism (as symbolism) of enchantment is a standard feature of post-industrial society and the associated cultural turn to "post-modernism" (Lyotard 1984; McLuhan 2006/1964, 313).

Game as trans-space

Following the academy's long-overdue engagement with videogames, there has been a surge in educing theory from them, with particularly strong examples including Poole (2000) and Juul (2005). The most recent attempt wires the videogame to the proliferation of digital space: "[a]ll games are digital. Without exception. They all come down to a strict decision: out or in, foul or fair, goal or no goal" (Wark 2007, 79). Like much of Wark's text, there is an emphasis on the surface, a refusal to treat the game and the gamer as anything other than a binary opposition. Wark's definition of the digital is clearly different to that of simultaneous projection and distancing outlined in this article, yet this approach decodes the concealed depths of the game, revealing "the game as a little cosmos of its own" (Riezler cited in Goffman 1961, 27). Using the definition of digital as outlined here, chess can be seen as a digital game – the distance between the player and the board is identified through the pieces, and the player summarily projects their will onto the game. However, the pieces are symbolic, both in the performative sense of changing the cosmos of the game-board, and in how both players relate to that world; they are trans-spatial in that they alter perception through the conception of the 64 squares, associated rules and interaction of the two players. It is also equally likely that the game will take place in the lived/perceived space of a kitchen, the perceived/conceived space of the street or the lived/digital space of an Internet site, the conceived/perceived space of the postal system, or even the purely enchanted space of the mind – as shown by Nabokov's (1964) elegiac novel *The Defence*. For a more vigorous game, such as squash, there are the rituals associated with preparation: the change of clothes, warming-up, use of scientific products such as clothing, racquets and drinks, perhaps even entering the orphic space of superstition in order to maintain perceived psychological advantage. Then, the player is ready to enter the conceived space of the court, dually perceived as a space of duel. Clearly, the individual is not only inhabiting many different spaces at once, but is transforming the self at the same time. In short, the game has inherent *meaning*, there is learnt behaviour – Merleau-Ponty's "motor-space" – that promotes understanding of the machinations and niceties of the game, even if the player *uses* the technology of the racquet, they are still aware of the importance of angles to the process and outcome of the game, showing that conceived spaces have meaning too. Ultimately, the game is based on a win/lose binary, but such a blunt assessment devalues the game and its special, but nevertheless quotidian, role in trans-space.

Videogames further extend the notion of the digital as they originate within that space of projection and distancing, but different types of technology demonstrate different levels of digital absorption. In a digital representation of chess, such as that played on a chess program, the technology employed is secondary to the game; chess is an elastic game and can be played in a variety of ways. For instance, chess played purely in the mind constitutes the "hot" medium of McLuhan, whereby the burden of interaction is undertaken by the individual player, whereas a "cooler" medium substitutes technology for interaction, as shown by a chess program such as *Deep Fritz 10* (ChessBase 2006). Early-era representations of commercial aviation such as *Kennedy Approach* (Hollis 1985) or *Solo Flight* (Meier 1983) also require the player to imagine part of the world that the game is unable to portray due to technical limitations. However, in the contemporary realm of amateur flight simulators, the medium takes the principal burden for the production of composite spaces – multiple monitors, a mocked-up cockpit containing real instruments, and even a briefing room connected to the cockpit via a skywalk – making flight simulation a cool medium, even if the majority of the tasks in the cockpit are undertaken by the pilot and co-pilot.

Pre-flight checks

The following is an ethnographic sketch of one of the largest, most sophisticated amateur flight simulators in the United Kingdom, undertaken during two visits to its location in the West Midlands during September 2006, the first of which was based on observation/ participation and the second on interviews with those involved. Made up of a 1/1 scale cockpit, all instruments are identical to those found in a Boeing 737-700 and are driven by six separate PCs running *Windows*, with a master computer operating *Microsoft Flight Simulator 1998* (Microsoft Games Studios 1997). The simulator is located in its own purpose-built extension on the side of the house and it took two years for the planning permission to be approved due to contention with West Midlands County Council as to whether the simulator comprised commercial use of domestic premises or not. Expecting George (names used within this paper are pseudonyms) to show some irritation at the intrusion of bureaucracy, it was actually a source of satisfaction, and he swelled with pride as he told me that: "professional simulators charge up to £500 per hour, which is not only a large amount of money, but is close to how much it costs to keep a real 737 in the air for an hour". His nephew, who flies 737-700s for the civil airline BMI, concurs, saying that: "it's as good as anything I've seen outside of industrial applications". In undertaking the building of a bespoke simulator George has come to realise the enormity of the project, which is still only 60% complete and is "more fun than the real thing, more accessible and more expensive ... it's all about the money, I've either got to save up and wait for money or wait for kit to be delivered from the US". With the final cost estimated to be around £90,000–100,000 and primarily financed by the sale of his electrical business, George is able to devote a great deal of time to the project due to his taking early retirement, but with 18 months still remaining until full completion, I was told by both Steve and George there would be "some champagne flowing on the first real flight!" – the celebratory tone reminiscent of a ship's maiden voyage or a housewarming.

The relationship between Steve and George is founded on happy coincidence, yet distinguished by hierarchy. They met when Steve delivered a piece of electrical equipment to George's house, where Steve saw *MS Flight Simulator* running on George's home PC. Both were fans of the series and, with this in mind, George outlined his plans for building a flight simulator, one of which they have previously constructed. The result is a symbiosis of the design and implementation process between the two men, with George modelling the hardware, such as the exterior of the cockpit, the skywalk and the briefing room, and Steve responsible for the networking of the seven on-board computers. The hierarchy is implicit, with George the *de facto* captain and Steve the first officer, with its basis evident in the location of the simulator (the lived space of George's house) and the amount of capital George invests in the project.

Flying in trans-space

It was a hot late September day as I walked into the house, through the kitchen where George's wife and son were drinking coffee and into the briefing room. Sequestered from the lived space of the house, the briefing room wall is replete with charts, showing flight paths, elapsed flight times, fuel requirements and weather forecasts. Exiting the briefing room and walking across the skywalk, the absorption becomes total. There is the soft hum of air conditioning in the cockpit and the accompanying wash of cool, dry air, reminding me of the "swoosh" of the pressurised cabin of *Airwolf*, one of my favourite television programmes when I was young. When I mentioned this, George accented: "I've always had an interest in aviation too, I miss things like *Take-Off* [a 1980s magazine-cum-journal devoted to aviation], but this is even closer than reading or watching even flying will ever take you, I'm *building* my own aircraft!" The pride is apparent in the detail; the fire extinguisher behind the first officer's chair, the flight computer and carpeting are all identical to those found in a 737-700.

The view out of the cockpit is an interesting melange of spaces. The transitional object of the windows are sanctioned Boeing products; double glazed and riveted to the fuselage, they provide a view onto a curved, cold-tube screen (to minimise overheating) that has the simulated environment of *Flight Simulator 1998* projected onto it. The simulator is built to "glass cockpit" specifications, a sophisticated innovation that negates the need for analogue instruments and a flight engineer, replacing them with a cornucopia of computers including navigation, engine and hydraulic management, known collectively as the "Flight Management System". George tells me this is beneficial: "not only does everything run smoother, but it somehow feels smoother, and of course there's more room for us without a wrench [engineer]". This smooth tactility is presumably due to the profusion of shiny blue screens showing artificial horizons and meteorological conditions that mimic the weather of any given place at any given time via connection to the Internet. Ultimately, through the windows and the screens – themselves driven by Microsoft's *Windows* – the cockpit becomes a transitional object, making the contingent space inside the cockpit almost cosy, a feeling complemented by George's wife bringing cups of tea for all of us, extending the lived space of the kitchen/home into the technological space of the digital/enchanted/perceived. Ostensibly, George's wife appeared as a stewardess in the cockpit, providing refreshment to those who cannot leave their conceived space due to the technical demands placed upon them. However, there is an explicit gender division operating here that is not limited to simulation: of the 11,661 people registered with Airline Transport Pilot Licences and therefore able to fly large commercial airliners, only 385 (3.3%) are women (United Kingdom Civil Aviation Authority 2007), suggesting that where the technical and conceived spaces of aviation are concerned, it is females who provide the emotional labour, with limited access to the executive power of the pilot, not only in the form of the everyday, due to curbs on admission to the flight deck, but structurally, with constraints on pursuing aviation as a career.

As George and Steve readied themselves for the first flight, it became apparent that the work-in-progress nature of the simulator meant that this flight would be somewhat different to a regular expedition. The lack of a throttle (for acceleration/deceleration) and a yoke (for control of roll, yaw and pitch) meant that the pilot and first officer could not fly the aircraft conventionally, but Steve informed me that it is still possible to fly a simulator – and by rote an airliner – by programming the Flight Management System and allowing the autopilot to fly, with corrections "dialled in" by the crew. The analogue terminology intrigued me; I believed that heading and speed would be inputted into the computer via a computerised interface with a numeric keypad. George showed me that while this would normally be the case during pre-flight, to directly alter the attitude and speed of the aircraft during flight requires the "dialling in" of direction and airspeed via mechanical sliders to minimise the potential for error. I was told that it is well known that many commercial flights can be flown entirely by autopilot from take-off until landing, although most pilots prefer to land "rudder and stick" (manually). In this flight the digital space of the autopilot would be at the behest of the aircrew, meaning that the flight relied on their perception of airspace and how this can be successfully transferred to the autopilot. The results were humorous and concomitantly dissonant.

Although the perception of being in a cockpit was slightly stymied by the lack of the sensory input of throttle and yoke, it was the manipulation of the mathematically conceived spaces of the flight computer that was most jarring. My perception was that the pilot and first officer would be seated and belted in their chairs, whereas they were both hunched over the Flight Management System in the left-hand corner of the cockpit, programming the proposed heading, altitude, speed and rate of climb/descent that instructs the autopilot of where to position the aeroplane in the conceived space of the flight path, as well as the digital space of the simulation. This, however, did give me the opportunity to sit in the first officer's chair on the right of the cockpit. It was my first time in the cockpit of a commercial airliner, and is infinitely more comfortable than that of a military aircraft, where the crew tend to fit around the technology. As the aircraft trundled onto the runway and then took off, it became clear that we were not climbing rapidly enough, and the trees at the end of the runway loomed large before a hasty reprogramming prevented any collision. After circling the airport, George and Steve attempted a landing on autopilot. Their perception of space was once again malign and the flight computer, which merely *uses* the coordinates without allowing for human error, promptly flew the aircraft into the ground, conceiving this to be the correct course of action. This is contrary to a human pilot who is believed to both correctly perceive and to have *learnt* to double-check the coordinates, although, as I later found out, this is not always the case. The reward for this perceived/conceived failure was the flooding of the windows of the cockpit with a graphical representation of a crashed Boeing 737. This is discordant as the space perceived by those in the cockpit remains the same (instruments, flight computers, headsets) but the individual is taken *outside* the body of the aircraft and the self to a point that George termed "buying the farm" (an aviation epigram for crashing a plane), with the individuals viewing the external digital husk of an aircraft while residing in the conceived internal space of the cockpit. Nevertheless, Steve refuted the malfunction of communication between spaces, "everything usually works smoothly and we don't have problems like this normally", with the lack of the tactile feedback of the throttle and yoke cited as the reason for the crash – demonstrating firstly the importance of co-construction of digital spaces with conception and perception; and, more unnervingly, what happens when these spaces grate rather than coalesce with each other.

Five-point landing

During my second visit I interviewed George and Steve about flying aeroplanes and how simulation matches to the world of commercial airliners. George was especially keen to tell me about the prevalence of virtual airlines.

> Virtual airlines are big business and have been around since the early nineties. These are firms with boards of directors and they task pilots to deliver airfreight from one side of the planet to the other. We have proper ATC [Air Traffic Control] and you've already seen the real-time weather updates. This is as real as it gets, a serious hobby with serious implications. (George)

When asked to elaborate on his final statement, Steve took up the story. "This is real money we're talking about here ... Qantas [Australian airline] were sued by a virtual airline for using their name on the net." Even though virtual airlines are not-for-profit organisations, impingement of trademarks is taken seriously as it affects their orientation within the simulated world. But this is not merely a one-way arrangement with the virtual airlines populating the business and capital spaces of commercial airliners.

> Telemetry from simulated flights can be used by manufacturers and airlines to improve safety and efficiency of their aircraft as well as their pilots ... it's not just the money, it's the safety of you and me, the passengers who use the airlines everyday. (Steve)

Steve then provided an example of the instance when George tested the discipline of his first officer by providing him with charts of an approach to Chicago's O'Hare airport.

> There is this famous tale of a pilot who was approaching Chicago O'Hare. It's a tricky
> approach because of the Rockies [mountain range], but nothing like Hong Kong used to be ...
> Anyway, George asked me to plot the [crash] course and program the autopilot, but I knew
> there was something up, he must think I'm bloody stupid! (Steve)

The actual flight incident had involved the pilot taking the wrong approach path,
resulting in a fatal crash. Clearly, there was a failure in the perception of the conceived
spatial areas, between the charts and airspace: a mistake Steve did not replicate.
Additionally, George told me of a Russian pilot who ignored the collision warnings given
out by the transponder of another aircraft, resulting in the fatalities of all onboard.

> This just shouldn't happen with autoland and ILS [instrument landing system]. You don't need
> to be able to see out of the cockpit to fly a plane ... a landing in pea-soup should be just as
> straightforward as on a day like today, although there are always other factors. (George)

These other factors are best illustrated by the story of a pilot whose 737 ran out of fuel,
but he was able to glide the aircraft to safety: a feat that has never been replicated in a
simulated environment. Steve elaborated: "the plane always ends up buying the farm in
simulation ... a real plane forms an 'edge' in an individual pilot which is difficult or nearly
impossible to simulate". The pressure of failure when a multitude of lives are endangered is
clearly a motivating factor in pilot performance, suggestive of an enchanted space that is
specific to the individual. Steve himself prefers to navigate purely through paper-based
charts as opposed to the digital space of the GPS to maintain this edge. In spite of the
limitations of simulation, there is still a link between edge and performance:

> You can do a long-haul flight and speed up the time spent in the air, [via the computer] but
> often the landing goes tits up on the pan [runway] ... I've lost count of the amount of times
> we've done that. It's not coherent, it doesn't feel right. I'd rather spend a real eight hours being
> bored and successful than two fake hours excited and dead. (Steve)

The perception of space occupied by the aircrew using the simulator is directly linked to
the passage of time and how this is seen to be coherent; clearly, a change in the perception
of time alters the perception of space, in neutral, negative and positive ways.

Conclusion: terminal building

The present article has shown how the concept of trans-space can be used to analyse the
nature of lives lived in twenty-first-century society: as a montage of movement between
eclectic spaces. The contemporary siting of spatial analysis requires the addition of two
typologies to Lefebvre's model – the enchanted and the digital – allowing for more subtle
distinctions between the triad of perceived, conceived and lived spaces. When applied to
the ethnographic data gathered from a flight simulator, trans-space can be seen to operate
as a practical concept: demonstrating the habitation of a number of different spaces at
once; the movement between these spaces; what happens when these spaces complement
each other; and what occurs when they work against one another. A literally crushing
example of this is seen in the decimation of symbols of the US's perceived economic and
military might by airliners in autumn 2001. Subsequent official investigation shows that
although at least one hijacker on each aircraft was Federal Aviation Authority-certificated
to fly large passenger jets, additional, or indeed, fundamental knowledge of aviation was
gleaned from "simulator training, readily available operational manuals, and perhaps, PC-
based simulator software" (National Commission on Terrorist Attacks Upon the United
States 2004, 5–6). The use of simulators is to train military pilots is orthodox practice, but
what was particularly chilling about 11 September 2001 was the ability to turn the

everyday, conceived space of civil aviation into a weapon via the digital, yet prosaic, software of flight simulation.

Further analysis of the complicity between spaces, the impact of time on space and *vice versa*, the link between simulation, play and learning and how contingent spaces affect game interaction are a few of the questions that a trans-spatial analysis of videogames will engage with in the future. Ultimately, it is hoped the model can offer an opportunity for examining videogames from the currently under-utilised perspective of spatial typology, and perhaps prompt and encourage wider understanding of this new and important area of academic study.

References

Augé, M. 1995. *Non-places: Introduction to an anthropology of supermodernity*. London: Verso.
Baudrillard, J. 1988. *The ecstasy of communication*. New York: Semiotext(e).
Broks, P. 2004. *Into the silent land*. London: Atlantic.
Castells, M. 1996. *The rise of the network society*. London: Blackwell.
Davis, E. 2004. *TechGnosis*. London: Serpent's Tail.
de Souza e Silva, A. 2006. From cyber to hybrid: Mobile technologies as interfaces of hybrid spaces. *Space and Culture* 9, no. 3: 261–78.
Elden, S. 2004. *Understanding Henri Lefebvre*. London: Continuum.
Goffman, E., 1961. *Encounters*. Indianapolis, IN: Bobbs-Merrill.
Haraway, D.J. 1991. *Simians cyborgs, and women: The reinvention of nature*. London: Free Association.
Hayles, N.K. 1999. *How we became posthuman: Virtual bodies in cybernetics, literature and informatics*. Chicago: University of Chicago Press.
Juul, J. 2005. *Half real: Videogames between real rules and fictional worlds*. Cambridge, MA: MIT Press.
Lefebvre, H. 1991. *The production of space*. Trans. Donald Nicholson-Smith. London: Blackwell.
———— 2006. *The critique of everyday life*. Vol. 3. Trans. Gregory Elliot. London: Verso.
Lloyd, J. 2003. Airport technology, travel and consumption. *Space and Culture* 6, no. 2: 93–109.
Lyotard, J.-F. 1984. *The postmodern condition: A report on knowledge*. Manchester: Manchester University Press.
McLuhan, M. 2006/1964. *Understanding media: The extensions of man*. Abingdon: Routledge.
Merleau-Ponty, M. 1962/1945. *Phenomenology of perception*. London: Routledge and Kegan Paul.
Muri, A. 2003. Of shit and the soul: Tropes of cybernetic disembodiment in contemporary culture. *Body and Society* 9, no. 3: 73–92.
Nabokov, V. 1964. *The defence*. London: Weidenfield and Nicolson.
National Commission on Terrorist Attacks Upon the United States. 2004. *Staff Statement No. 4*. http://govinfo.library.unt.edu/911/staff_statements/staff_statement_4.pdf (accessed 8 January 2008).
Poole, S. 2000. *Trigger happy: The inner life of videogames*. London: Fourth Estate.
Shields, R. 1999. *Lefebvre, love and struggle: Spatial dialectics*. London: Routledge.
Soja, E. 1996. *Thirdspace*. London: Blackwell.
United Kingdom Civil Aviation Authority. 2007. Licence breakdown by age and sex. Pers. commun. with Dave Davies, Personnel Licensing Department, 24 July 2007.
Urry, J. 2000. *Sociology beyond societies*. London: Routledge.
Wark, M. 2007. *Gamer theory*. Cambridge, MA: Harvard University Press..

Gameography

ChessBase. 2006. *Deep Fritz 10*. Hamburg: ChessBase.
Hollis, A. 1985. *Kennedy approach*. Birmingham, UK: MicroProse/US Gold.
Linden Lab. 2003. *Second life*. San Francisco, CA: Linden Research.
Microsoft Games Studios. 1997. *Microsoft Flight Simulator 1998*. Redmond, WA: Microsoft.
Meier, S. 1983. *Solo flight*. Birmingham, UK: MicroProse/US Gold.

Dispreferred actions and other interactional breaches as devices for occasioning audience laughter in television "sitcoms"

Elizabeth Stokoe

The present paper uses conversation analysis to examine a hitherto unexplored aspect of the interactional production of humour. Taking sequences of talk from the American television sitcom *Friends*, it analyses the way breaches of the "generic orders of conversational organization", including preference organization and turn-taking, function as devices for occasioning audience laughter. The analysis further reveals that it is not just breaches themselves that make laughter relevant, but the juxtaposition of normatively "appropriate" and "inappropriate" methods for doing dispreferred turns within the same course of action (e.g. contrasted invitation–declination and apology–acceptance adjacency pairs). Although the data are fictional, they are constructed by people who apply mundane knowledge about talk's organization and rely on their audience to do the same in response. This modern, mediated form of "breaching experiment" provides a vehicle for understanding the activities through which everyday social life is practically accomplished.

Introduction

The present paper uses conversation analysis to examine a hitherto unexplored aspect of the interactional production of humour. Taking sequences of conversation from the American television sitcom *Friends*, the article analyses the way "breaches" of conversational "rules" function as devices for eliciting laughter from the audience.

Let us start with a scene from an episode in which two characters, Monica and Phoebe, are having a conversation in the apartment Monica shares with another character, Rachel. In Extract 1 over the page, "A" is the audience, or laughter track. A basic question about this sequence is what accounts for the audience laughter (line 7). It is not occasioned by the telling of a formulaic joke: the humour is "spontaneous" (Mulkay 1988), created by Phoebe's response to Monica's prior utterance. At lines 1–3, Monica is crossing the apartment to where Phoebe is sitting. She greets Phoebe ("Hey Pheebs"), nominating her as co-participant in the ensuing talk, and Phoebe raises her head in response. Monica's next turn ("Y'know what I'm thinki:n'?") is a "pre-announcement" or "pre-telling", an action designed to get a "go-ahead" from Phoebe for Monica to report her thoughts on some unspecified topic. For comparison, consider Extract 2 overleaf, from the start of an

Extract 1. Season 2: The One With Ross's New Girlfriend

1   M: Hey Pheebs.

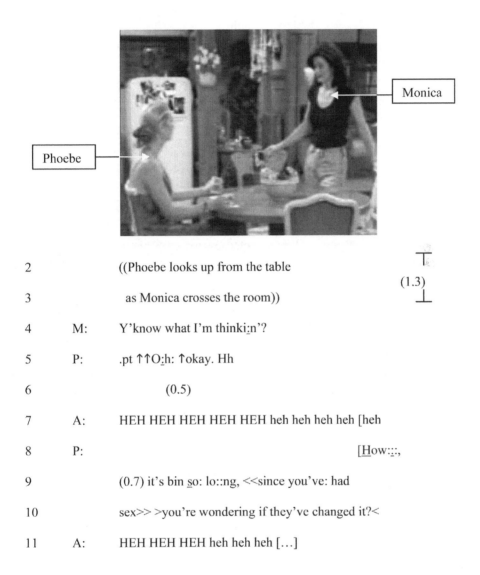

2   ((Phoebe looks up from the table

3   as Monica crosses the room))   (1.3)

4   M: Y'know what I'm thinki:n'?

5   P: .pt ↑↑O:h: ↑okay. Hh

6   (0.5)

7   A: HEH HEH HEH HEH HEH heh heh heh heh [heh

8   P: [How:::,

9   (0.7) it's bin so: lo::ng, <<since you've: had

10   sex>> >you're wondering if they've changed it?<

11   A: HEH HEH HEH heh heh heh […]

ordinary telephone call, which shows how pre-announcements occur and are routinely responded to. Donny's pre-announcement ("Guess what.") is receipted by Marcia's partial repeat of the question word uttered in Donny's turn ("What."). This "go-ahead" returns the floor to Donny, who then delivers the news about his car.

Returning to Extract 1, Phoebe's response to Monica's "pre" ("↑↑O:h: hokay. Hh") is fitted to the form but not the function of Monica's turn: it is not a "go-ahead". Rather, it treats Monica's turn as an invitation to guess what she is thinking, rather than as a "pre" to Monica's own report. The "↑↑O:h:" displays Phoebe's (mis)comprehension of the project of Monica's turn, and "↑okay." aligns with it. The gap at line 6, and audience laughter at

Extract 2. MDE: "Stalled"

1			((phone rings))
2	M:	Hello?	
3	D:	H'lo <u>Ma</u>rsha,	
4	M:	Y<u>e</u>:a[h.]	
5	D:		[It's D]onny.
6	M:	<u>Hi</u> Do:nny.	
7	D: →	Guess what. hh	
8	M: →	What.	
9	D: →	.hh my c<u>a</u>:r is st<u>a</u>::lled.	

line 7, both mark this response as in some way inapposite. As the laughter subsides, Phoebe formulates a candidate answer to Monica's question, displaying that she is "searching" for a response in the slow-paced delivery of the first part of her turn ("<u>H</u>ow:::, (0.7) it's bin so: lo::ng, ≪since you've: had sex≫") and speeding up as her answer progresses (">you're wondering if they've changed it? <"). The laughter that follows her answer is responsive to a different type of breach to do with the norms of discussing someone's intimate fears and sex life.

In writing this scene, the scriptwriters display mundane knowledge, as members of a culture, about how pairs of turns are normatively ordered. Monica's first turn ("Y'know what I'm thinki:n'?") is the "first pair part" (FPP) of an "adjacency pair". An adjacency pair is the basic unit of sequence construction, from which courses of action are built. After one speaker has done a first action, their recipient is expected to respond with a turn that delivers a second action paired with, and fitted to, the first one (e.g. "invitation–acceptance"). Producing a FPP makes a second "conditionally relevant"; that is, anything produced next is inspectable and accountable as an instance of that second pair part. So, on issuing an invitation, any response to it will be hearable as relevant to it, as being an acceptance, rejection, stalling manoeuvre, account for non-acceptance, or whatever. As Heritage (2005, 105) explains:

> by producing next actions, participants show an understanding of a prior action … e.g., by an acceptance, someone can show an understanding that a prior turn was complete, that it was addressed to them, that it was an action of a particular type (e.g., an invitation), and so on. These understandings are (tacitly) confirmed or can become the objects of repair at any third turn in an ongoing sequence. Through this process they become mutual understandings created through a sequential architecture of intersubjectivity.

This kind of interest in the way interaction works is an ethnomethodological, conversation analytic interest. "Ethnomethodology", the "study of people's methods", was invented by sociologist Harold Garfinkel (1967). A central concern of ethnomethodology was to make "commonsense" studyable, by analysing "everyday activities as members' methods for making those same activities visibly-rational-and-reportable-for-all-practical-purposes; that is, 'accountable'" (Garfinkel 1967, vii). To interrogate the "seen but unnoticed" organization of social life, Garfinkel conducted "breaching experiments". In one experiment, he instructed his students to engage friends in conversation and ask them to "clarify the sense of his [sic] commonplace remarks" (1967, 42). The following is a reported conversation from one of the students conducting the experiment (from Garfinkel 1967, 42–43).

(Subject)	How is your girlfriend feeling?
(Experimenter)	What do you mean, "How is she feeling?" Do you mean physical or mental?
(Subject)	I mean how is she feeling? What's the matter with you? (He looked peeved).
(Experimenter)	Nothing. Just explain a little clearer what do you mean?
(Subject)	Skip it. How are your Med School applications coming?
(Experimenter)	What do you mean, "How are they?"
(Subject)	You know what I mean.
(Experimenter)	I really don't.
(Subject)	What's the matter with you? Are you sick?

In each turn, the experimenter (E) attempts to get the subject (S) to define explicitly turns that would usually be treated as having a readily understandable meaning. As in this example, subjects' responses to experimenters were often hostile, although they sometimes treated the experimenter as being designedly funny. Like the *Friends* data, then, when speakers do not respond in expectable ways, one possible outcome is laughter. Garfinkel's breaching experiments allowed him to "detect some expectancies that lend commonplace scenes their familiar, life-as-usual character" (1967, 37), a notion taken up by Schegloff (1968), who showed in his analysis of telephone call openings how the comprehensibility of "normal scenes" was illuminated "by considering disruption of them" (Schegloff 1968, 1077). This paper will demonstrate further ways through which interactional "breaches" reveal the generic orders that enable them to be understood *as* breaches, and recognized by audiences as legitimate occasions for laughter.

Humour, interaction and the media

There are massive, interdisciplinary literatures on humour and laughter, and on the media, but few studies analyse the actual interaction of television sitcoms beyond the jokes that are told within them (for example, Bubel and Spitz 2006). Neither is anything written specifically about the current topic: that is, interaction-order breaches as devices for occasioning laughter. Elsewhere, there are numerous theoretical accounts of "what makes something funny" and the role of humour in social life (for example, Billig 2005; Mulkay 1988), analyses of the narrative, semantic and pragmatic structure of "jokes" and the cognitive competencies required to understand them (for example, Attardo and Raskin 1991), the function of humour for solidarity-building and in-group membership (for example, Coates 2007), and the turn-by-turn organization of "conversational joking" in everyday talk (cf. Norrick 1993; Sacks 1992).

Conversation analysts have focused less on "humour" as a unit of analysis than on "laughter" and its organization and function in everyday and institutional talk (for an overview, see Glenn 2003). One basis of conversation analytic studies is to understand laughter as an action-oriented, recipient-designed feature of interaction, rather than as a psycho-physiological, uncontrollable response to an inner cognitive–emotional state. For example, speakers regularly laugh through reporting troubles or making complaints to show they are in a position to take it lightly (for example, Edwards 2005; Jefferson 1984), patients laugh when dealing with delicate matters at the doctor's (for example, Haakana 2001), and people use laughter to mitigate potential disagreement in meetings (for example, Osvaldsson 2004).

Sitcoms have previously been studied in terms of their constitutive features, influence and legacy, as vehicles for understanding social change, for their relevance to particular audiences, and with regards to genre and intertextuality (for example, Mills 2005). Many researchers have investigated the way sitcoms undermine or reinforce stereotypes of gender, age, class, race and sexuality (for example, Rockler's [2006] study of the representation of Jewish identity in *Friends*). The current paper makes a novel contribution to the existing literature on television comedy, and on understanding how humour works more generally, by examining how laughter is occasioned by *interactional* breaches or transgressions, rather than by joke-telling, wordplay or transgressions of "what is socially respectable or ethically correct" (Littlewood and Pickering 1998, 292). Instead, this paper will show how the audience's laughter turns on transgressions of the "generic orders of organization in talk-in-interaction" (Schegloff 2007, xiii).

Data and method

Friends is an American television sitcom about six friends – Rachel, Monica, Phoebe, Ross, Chandler and Joey – living in New York. Ten seasons ran between 1994 and 2004, and repeats still fill television schedules all over the world. I developed my initial observation about "interactional breaches" when using *Friends* data to teach conversation analysis to postgraduate students. As Bubel and Spitz (2006, 71) comment, the study of scripted interaction can yield insights "into underlying knowledge about real conversation" (see also McHoul's [1987] paper on the use of conversation analysis to analyse fictional conversation in literary texts). The data presented represent just a handful of examples of the phenomenon under investigation. I transcribed each extract[1] according to Jefferson's (2004) conventions for conversation analysis (CA), which pay attention to the pacing, prosodic and turn-organizational features of interaction. The CA findings and concepts on which the analysis draws will be explained as they become relevant to the analytic commentary.

Analysis

Extract 3 comes from the pilot episode.[2] Rachel (RA) has arrived in New York seeking her old friend Monica, after abandoning her wedding and leaving her fiancé at the altar. Monica's brother Ross (RO), also newly single, is moving into a new apartment. Ross asks Rachel if she wants to come to his apartment with two of the other friends, Joey and Chandler, to put together furniture.

The basic activity in this scene is Ross's invitation to Rachel to come with Joey and Chandler to help put together his furniture. At line 1, Ross launches the sequence with a "pre-invitation" ("So Rachel what're you uh: what're you up to tonight."); readily recognizable as leading up to a possible invitation. Responses to such preliminaries "display the stance the responder is taking up toward the action to which the question was preliminary" (Schegloff 2007, 29). If an invitation is welcome, the answer to the pre-invitation should be, as in the above example, "↑no:thin(h)g.". One function of pre-sequences is to help the speaker who might issue an invitation avoid rejection. Or, more technically, "to help the interaction avoid a sequence with a rejected base FPP", or "first pair part" in an adjacency pair of actions (Schegloff 2007, 31). Rachel could therefore respond to Ross by reporting that she has plans for the evening, "blocking" the invitation being issued. Although Rachel gives a "go-ahead" response " ↑no:thin(h)g.", its formulation as an ironic

Extract 3. Season 1: Pilot

1	RO:	So R̲achel what're you uh: what're you up to tonight.
2		(0.6)
3	RA:	We:ll, I was ki̲:nda supposed t'be headed for Aru̲:ba
4		on my h:oneymoon.=so ↑no̲:thin(h)g. uh heh
5	A:	HEH HEH HEH HEH heh heh heh heh heh heh
6	RO:	Ri̲:ght. you're not even (0.2) ~getting your
7		honeymoon.~
8	RO:	God
9		(0.3)
10	RO:	↑No. no although .pch Aru̲:ba. hheh this time of
11		year? ffehr: Talk about your: (1.8) big
12		li̲zards,
13	A:	HEH HEH HEH HEH heh heh heh heh heh [heh heh heh]
14	RO:	[Anyway if you:]
15	→	if you don't feel like being ↑alone tonight, uh Joey
16	→	an' Chandler are comin' over to help me put together
17	→	my: my new furniture.

Ross

Chandler and Joey

Rachel

18	C:	Yes an' we're (0.2) <u>v</u>ery excited [ab<u>o</u>:ut it,
19	A:	[HEH HEH HEH HEH
20		heh heh heh heh heh heh
21	RA: →	Well <u>a</u>ctually thanks: but I think I'm jus' gonna:
22		hang out (0.3) here tonight.=it's- (.) been a long
23		[day.
24	RO:	[Oh <u>s</u>ure okay.=sure.
25		(0.2)
26	J: →	Hey <u>Ph</u>eebs.=you wanna help?
27		(0.3)
28	P: →	↑Oh:: ↑I wish I <u>c</u>ould but I don't want to.
29		(0.3)
30	A: →	HEH [HEH HEH HEH heh heh heh heh heh heh

| 31 | J: | [(('okay' gesture; Joey nods and looks bemused)) |

upshot of the day's emotional circumstances adds to the inapposite nature of Ross's "pre": he has asked her what she is "up to" on the night of her abandoned wedding, while she sits in front of him in her wedding dress. It also sets up the conditions for a possible rejection later. This response, and Ross's next turn (an attempt to minimize the positive aspects of the honeymoon), is also designed to receive laughter.

Having received Rachel's "go-ahead", Ross issues his invitation, the "base FPP" that was projected by the pre-invitation (line 14). Before Rachel's "second pair part", however, is another pair of turns: an ironic comment from Chandler about the prospective DIY, and audience laughter (lines 18–20). This inserted adjacency pair explicitly includes the audience: the FPP is a "joke", and the second pair part is "laughter" (Norrick 1993). However, what is interesting is the contrast between Ross's invitation and Rachel's response, which turns out to be a declination, and the subsequent invitation–declination adjacency pair in which Phoebe declines Joey's invitation to join them in the DIY (lines 26–28). Phoebe's declination, in contrast to Rachel's, prompts laughter. So what is the audience laughing at, at line 30, that it is not at lines 24–25?

To answer this question we need to understand that adjacency pairs are analysable in terms of their "preference organization". If pre-sequences like Ross's pre-invitation are designed to avoid rejection of a subsequent invitation, then this tells us something about possible responses to invitations: they can be accepted or declined. These are not symmetrical, equally valued alternatives. A "plus" or preferred response to an invitation will promote the successful accomplishment of the course of action, or project, embodied in the FPP; that is, it will accept it (Schegloff 2007, 59–60). A "minus" or dispreferred response will decline it. Pomerantz (1984) has shown that whereas preferred responses are often short and "unaccountable", dispreferred responses are "marked" and "mitigated": they are more elaborate turns that often follow a gap, they may be prefaced with turn-initial delays like "well" and contain pauses and other signs of "perturbation", and may contain accounts for why the speaker cannot produce the preferred response.

Rachel's response to Ross's invitation, then, as a declination, is dispreferred. It contains many of the features listed above: it is prefaced with "well", it contains an appreciation of the invitation ("actually thanks:"), and an account for the rejection that reinstates her earlier response to Ross's pre-invitation (i.e. abandoning her wedding means "it's- (.) been a long day."). Formulated this way, there is no breach: Rachel produces a mitigated dispreferred response. Ross's reply is a "no trouble" closure of the sequence ("Oh sure okay. =sure.").

This invitation–declination sequence contrasts sharply with the second, launched by Joey at line 26. He asks Phoebe if she wants "to help", which functions to invite her to go to Ross's apartment (i.e. he is not *himself* asking for help). The first part of Phoebe's reply, "↑Oh:: ↑I wish I could but", looks like the start of a standard dispreferred turn, showing appreciation of the invitation before declining it. But the second part, "I don't want to.", although it accounts for the rejection, is not the sort of inability account generally found in declinations, used to fend off the notion that speakers *cannot*, rather than *do not want to*, accept the invitation (Drew 1984). In ordinary conversation, such a turn might be treated as argumentative, and sanctioned by the next speaker ("What's the matter with *you*?"). As Schegloff (2007, 73n) notes, conflict may develop when parties abandon doing dispreferred responses and instead "formulate their positions and stances in unmitigated and full-blooded forms ...". However, the next turn is laughter from the audience alongside Joey's bemused, embodied "okay" gesture (line 31). His response ends the sequence and its quality is as a light-hearted assessment of "typical" Phoebe. As evidenced in Extract 1, Phoebe is an eccentric character whose humour is often based in these sorts of interactional breaches.

By writing this scene, and by laughing at the place designed for laughter, the scriptwriters and their recipients display mundane knowledge of preference organization and the way social actions are accomplished, turn by turn, in talk. Whether the audience laughter is "real" or "canned", its precise location after Phoebe delivers an unmitigated dispreferred action produces her action *as* a joke, *as* a breach, and so is an integral part of the interaction. The fact that Phoebe's declination immediately follows Rachel's demonstration of the "appropriate" way to turn down an invitation provides a contrast with, and a further contextual basis for, seeing the subsequent breach as funny.

Extract 4 also comes from the pilot episode. It occurs at the end of the programme, during which the audience has learnt that Ross has long-standing, unrequited romantic feelings for Rachel. Here, he tells her that he wanted to be her boyfriend when they were still at school.

Extract 4. Season 1: Pilot

1	RO:	You know you pro:ba'ly didn't know this but back in
2		high school I had ā um: (0.5) .tch (0.6) major:
3		(0.2) crush on you. Hhh
4		(1.6)

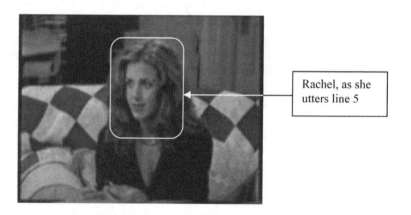

Rachel, as she utters line 5

5	RA:	°I knew. hh°
6		(1.0)
7	RO:	You di:d. Oh:'kay. .hh
8		(1.8)
9	RO:	I always figured you jus' thought I was Monica's
10		geeky older bro:ther.
11		(0.9)
12	RA:	I di:d.
13		(0.2)
14	RO:	O:h.

Ross, as he
utters line 14

15   A: HEH HEH HEH HEH HEH HEH heh heh heh heh heh heh

The scene starts with Ross telling Rachel about the crush he had on her at school. He formulates his telling with the preface "you pro:ba'ly didn't know this but". That this is a delicate matter is displayed in the way Ross delivers his disclosure (note the pauses, "um:" and ".tch") and in Rachel's delayed, softly uttered response ("°I knew. hh°"). Her response is minimal, focusing on the "no news" aspect of his turn rather than on the fact that he had a crush on her (an alternative response might contain an acknowledgement and an assessment, e.g. "I knew and it was really sweet", or else a reciprocal self-disclosure). It also disconfirms Ross's prediction that she did not know about his crush on her, and in that sense is dispreferred, but mitigated in a way that handles Ross's potential embarrassment.

After receipting Rachel's minimal acknowledgement ("You di:d. Oh:'kay."), Ross formulates an account for why he thought Rachel did not know about his crush: "I always figured you jus' thought I was Monica's geeky older bro:ther." (lines 9–10). This account contains a self-deprecating, self-assessment. Generally, the preferred response to an assessment is agreement, but, as Pomerantz (1984, 77–78) demonstrates, the preferred response to a self-deprecating assessment is *disagreement* because agreement would amount "to the second speaker's criticism of his or her co-participant". Thus Rachel's response ("I di:d.") to the self-deprecation is a second dispreferred action. Ross's responses to both these dispreferred turns display a "change of state" (Heritage 1984): a revision of what he thought he knew with regards to Rachel's stance toward him ("O:h."). But note that audience laughter follows the *second*, not the first, of Rachel's dispreferred turns. This is because the first is delivered in a way that mitigates the dispreferred action, whereas the second is delivered "bluntly". Furthermore, the humour is provided for not *just* by the unmitigated delivery of the second dispreferred, but by the *contrast* between the two pairs of actions, much like the contrasted invitation–declination sequences in Extract 3.

Extract 5 comes from an episode that introduces a new character, Danny. Earlier in the story, Rachel and Monica are looking for kitchen equipment in their building's storeroom when the lights go out, and they see a hairy figure looming out of the darkness. Scared, they "fog" him with a "bug bomb". They later discover that the figure was Danny, who recently moved into their building after a trek in the Andes. Rachel and Monica go to apologize.

Extract 5. Season 5: The One With The Yeti

1	R:	((knocks on door))
2	A:	HEH heh heh
3	D:	((opens door))
4	D:	>Yeh.<
5	R:	↑Hi. ((clears throat)) <u>Y</u>ou might not remember us.

Danny, with his 'Yeti' beard

Monica and Rachel at Danny's door

6	R:	but <u>we</u> are the girls that fogged you. uh heh [heh]=
7	M:	[heh]=
8	A:	[heh]=
9	R:	=[heh]
10	M:	=[heh]
11	A:	=[heh heh [heh]
12	M:	[£We're-] we're really sorry we fogged
13		you. hh
14	R:	£Yeh.£ hhh
15	M:	°ye(h)h°
16	D:	.pt >>Okay.<< ((closes door))
17	A:	HEH HEH HEH HEH heh heh heh heh heh heh

Rachel and Monica at line 18

18	R:	Hmm ((looking affronted, knocks on door again))
19	A:	Heh heh heh heh heh heh
20	D:	((opens door))
21	R:	↑Hi. .hh uh: ↑jus' so you know: we- we didn't <u>me:an</u>
22		to fo:g you.=We- we <u>actually</u> thought you were like a
23		<u>Ye</u>ti £or£ s(h)o(h)m(h)e(h)[t(h)h(h)i(h)n(h)g. heh
24	M:	[heh heh [heh heh
25	A:	[HEH HEH HEH HEH
26		heh heh heh heh heh [heh
27	D:	[>Okay.< [(((closes door))
28	A:	[HEH HEH HEH HEH heh
29		heh heh [°heh heh heh heh heh heh heh heh heh heh°]=
30	R:	[((thumps on door))]=
31	A:	=[°heh heh heh heh heh heh heh heh heh heh heh°]=
32	D:	[(((opens door)) Ye:::s,]
33	A:	=[°heh HEH heh heh heh°]
34	R:	[↑Hi. ((clears throat))] <u>sorry</u> to <u>bother</u> you.=but
35		↑I don't think <u>we</u> can ac<u>cept</u> your ac<u>cept</u>ance of our
36		apology.=it ↑just doesn't really seem like you <u>mean</u>
37		it.

38	M:	°Myeh.°
39		(1.4)
40	D:	<Ohkay.> ((closes door))
41	A:	HEH HEH HEH HEH heh heh heh heh heh [heh] heh
42	M:	[Whow.]
43	M:	↑That ↑guy is so ↑ru̲:de.
44	R:	Re̲hally.
45		(0.2)
46	R:	↑What is ↑↑with that guy.
47		(0.6)
48	R:	>I mean< ↑you'd ↑forgive me if I fogged yo̲:u,
49	A:	Heh heh heh heh heh [°heh heh heh heh heh heh heh°]=
50	M:	[Well you ↑di:d a little bit,]
51	A:	=HEH heh heh heh heh heh
52	R:	↑↑Ohh ↑↑my ↑↑Ghod.=↑↑Honey ↑I'm ↑so ↑so̲:rry.
53		(0.5)
54	M:	.hh £↑I ↑to̲tally ↑forgi̲:ve you[::.£
55	R:	[↑Really?
56	A:	[HEH HEH HEH HEH HEH
57		heh [heh heh HEH HEH HEH HEH HEH HEH HEH HEH HEH

Rachel and Monica at line 58

| 58 | M: | [((nods and they hug each other)) |

The humour turns on the contrast between types of responses to apologies. Rachel and Monica's apology ("£We're- we're really sorry we fogged you.") and account for "fogging" Danny ("We- we actually thought you were like a Ye̲ti £or£ s(h)o(h)m(h)e(h)[t(h)h(h)i(h)n(h)g.") are first pair parts of adjacency-pair sequences. The preferred response to an apology is one that promotes "social solidarity by somehow *mitigating or undermining an apology's claim to have caused offense*" (Robinson 2004, 302). In other words, recipients accept apologies and downplay or eliminate, rather than endorse, any offensive actions. The two most common responses, "That's all right" and "That's okay", are often followed by "statements that mitigate, and sometimes overtly deny, an apology's claim to have caused offense" such as "no problem" (Robinson 2004, 303).

·   With regards to the preference organization of apologies, Danny's response is complicated. " »Okay. «" accepts Monica's apology (line 16), but there is no indexical term (e.g. "that's") in his formulation, which truncates it. This truncation works in aggregate with its speeded-up delivery and Danny's door-closing action to produce an abrupt, and possibly dispreferred, turn. Further evidence that " »Okay. «" is dispreferred comes from two subsequent turns. First, in Rachel's response (line 18), she looks "affronted", summons Danny again, and provides an account for the "fogging" – in *pursuit* of the preferred acceptance response (lines 21–23). Second, between Danny's " »Okay. «" and Rachel's account comes the audience's laughter (line 17), occasioned by Danny's breach of the rule regarding responses to apologies. Danny receipts Rachel's account by recycling his response to the initial apology (" >Okay. <" plus door-closing, line 27). This gets further laughter from the audience and another round of door-knocking from Rachel. Danny opens the door, saying "Ye:::s," (line 32), which Rachel treats as a "new" greeting by reciprocating it (line 34). This time she does not pursue an apology acceptance but complains about Danny's "acceptance" of their apology because "it ↑just doesn't really seem like you mean it.". In so doing, Rachel, with support from Monica (line 38), makes explicit *what kind of breach this is* by formulating it. After a gap, Danny recycles his abrupt response once more to close his part in the sequence (line 40).

Two further sequences occur before the end of the scene. First, Rachel and Monica collaboratively assess Danny's actions, again making explicit what kind of breach has occurred ("↑That ↑guy is so ↑ru:de.", "↑What is ↑↑with that guy."), before doing another apology-acceptance sequence when it turns out Rachel accidentally "fogged" Monica (lines 50–58). Rachel treats as shocking the news that she "fogged" Monica ("↑↑Ohh ↑↑my ↑↑Ghod. ="), and prefaces her subsequent apology with a term of endearment ("↑↑ Honey"). The apology itself contains an intensifier ("↑I'm ↑so ↑so:rry.") and is delivered with markedly raised pitch, which works cumulatively with the lexical content to produce an unambiguous apology. Monica's apology acceptance is grammatically and prosodically fitted to Rachel's apology ("£↑I ↑*totally* ↑forgi:ve you::.£"), and delivers an unambiguous preferred response. The scene ends with Rachel and Monica hugging. Like Extracts 3 and 4, the humour turns on a *contrast* between methods for delivering dispreferred actions; here, an exaggerated contrast between "appropriate" and "inappropriate" ways to receipt apologies, and their social–relational implications. Danny's performance is "unfriendly" throughout, and markedly mismatched with regard to Monica and Rachel. He neither aligns with their apology nor their formulation of events as humorous (note the post-utterance laughter particles, "smiley voice" and interpolated laughter at lines 6, 14, and 21–23).

The final extract, Extract 6, illustrates a different kind of breach to those seen thus far in the paper: a breach of turn-taking organization, rather than of adjacency and preference organization. Monica wants a baby but has no partner. She has decided to visit a sperm bank, and Ross is trying to discourage her. At line 1, Monica has not finished her turn when Ross starts talking in overlap at line 2. As in Extract 5, in which Danny's apology acceptance was explicitly formulated as a breach, Ross's interruptive violation of turn-taking is similarly formulated in Monica's reprimand ("↑lips moving ↑still talking."). This occasions laughter from the audience, and at line 6 Monica restarts the turn launched at line 1, recycling her original words ("It may not be ide:al …").

To generate this sequence, Ross must begin speaking at a point where Monica has not signalled that her turn may be possibly complete. The mundane competence needed to accomplish this is formalized in Sacks, Schegloff, and Jefferson's (1974) article on turn-taking. When Ross starts talking, Monica is in the midst of an incomplete "turn constructional unit" (TCU),[3] at least in terms of its prosodic shape, which has not yet completed the action it projects. A clear point of possible completion, or "transition relevance place" (TRP), arrives on the word "something."; when the sentence is complete, Monica's pitch falls to terminal, and a recognizable action has been accomplished. However, Ross may be exploiting a possible TRP after "way": coming in at this point treats Monica as accepting that a sperm donor is not ideal, and competes for the next turn so that he can sequentially delete or head off her defensive account. Sacks et al. also show how speakers are normatively entitled to one TCU in a turn – which means that taking a multiple TCU turn, as Monica is doing, entails methods for keeping the floor beyond the TRP. Monica demonstrates one such method, latching a second TCU immediately onto

Extract 6. Season 3: The One with the Jam

```
1       M:      So ↑this ↑isn't the ideal way t'[do something.=<bu-]=

2       R:                                      [ Oh it's not the      ]=

3       M:      =[ .hh ↑lips moving] ↑still talking.

4       R:      =[ideal way (of it?)]
```

Monica's gesture at line 3

```
5       A:      HEH HEH HEH HEH heh heh [heh heh

6       M:                              [It may not be ide:al but-

7               (0.5) hhh I'm shho ready.
```

the first (" = <bu-") to "rush past" the TRP. However, she halts the second TCU at "bu-" to insert her admonishment of Ross for talking when she has not finished her turn.

Concluding remarks

This paper has examined a device used by scriptwriters to generate laughter in television sitcoms based on members' knowledge of, and mundane competence in, the interactional organization of conversation. It has shown how audience laughter may be occasioned by breaches of such organization, including of turn-taking, adjacency and preference. For example, laughter regularly followed dispreferred actions that were delivered without their normative mitigation-oriented features. And, as several extracts have demonstrated, it was not just the breaches themselves that occasioned laughter, but the *juxtaposition* of normatively "appropriate" and "inappropriate" methods for doing dispreferred turns within the same course of action (e.g. invitation–declination and apology–acceptance adjacency pairs).

It is perhaps a result of how "rude" these breaches would seem (as reported in Garfinkel's breaching experiments) that examples from "real" conversation are difficult to find. As Robinson (2004), 315) observes, "examples of unambiguously dispreferred responses are extremely rare ... given their threat to a relationship specifically, and to social harmony generally". However, consider the following final fragment of "real" data, Extract 7, that comes from my collection of heterosexual couples on first "speed" dates. The woman (F) is telling the man (M) the qualities she finds attractive in a prospective partner. At line 2, M produces the continuer "Myeh," as F searches to select words for her list. F continues to produce the list over two more turns, sequentially deleting the gaps that develop between them at lines 3 and 5 by indicating that she is still in the midst of ("Um:::") and continuing ("An'") her action. In other words, M's lack of response at lines 3 and 5, where he might have done another continuer, or begun his own list, is oriented to and treated by F as space for her continued action, rather than his non-response. Keeping the interactional wheels turning, rather than drawing attention to a co-participants' lack of response, might be important in this kind of dating interaction. At line 6, F completes her list. M's response is a confirmatory repeat of the final item "An' loyal". Notably, then, via this turn and previous non-uptakes, M appears to be resisting saying much about his own likes and dislikes, and it is in this environment that our target breach occurs.

Following M's repeated receipt of her list item, F invites M to produce his own list ("whaddabout you.",). As a *question*, the preferred response is an *answer*. What would fit the affiliative progress of the sequence is reciprocal list. However, after a short gap, M says "Yes." (line 11). This is an ambiguous response. It could be an agreement with F's list (i.e. "Yes, all of those"). But F's question was a "wh-" question, not a "yes–no interrogative", which makes M's one-word response not fitted to the question's format. And F treats it as such by producing a "repair initiator" indicative of trouble ("£E(h)h?£"), but also by laughing through her reply. So she treats his response as both puzzling and as a candidate attempt at humour. After a longer gap develops (line 13), F launches a new sequence, interpreting the silence as evidence that there is nothing more to come from M.

Here, then, M produces a dispreferred, or at least inapposite, response, which is ambiguous as to its action-orientation, and therefore with regards to its status as a breach. F's laughter functions to mitigate M's actions, treating it as possibly funny rather than disagreeable. Treating candidate "breaches" of interactional norms as funny is one method members can use to avoid conflict, seen in these "real" data, in Garfinkel's experiments, and in scripted interaction. This is a potential topic for further investigation. Until then,

Extract 7. SD-5

```
1        F:        Sense of humour::[:        ] intelligence.=good fu::n

2        M:                          [Myeh,]

3                          (0.8)

4        F:        Um::::

5                          (1.1)

6        F:        An' loyal.

7        M:        An' loyal.

8                          (0.3)

9        F         Yeh: an' whaddabout you.

10                         (0.2)

11       M: →      Yes.

12       F: →      £E(h)h?£ .hh ↑heh ↑heh ↑heh .hhh

13                         (0.6)

14       F:        Where d'you come from originally then.
```

the present paper has shed light on the complex relationship between laughter and social action. Its data may be fictional, but these scripts are constructed by members who apply mundane knowledge about normative practices and rely on their audience to do the same in response. This modern, mediated form of "breaching experiment", like Garfinkel's original studies, is a productive vehicle for understanding the activities through which everyday social life is practically accomplished.

Acknowledgements

The author is grateful to Michael Billig, Christy Bird, Derek Edwards, Susan Speer, Clare Stockill and the editors for their helpful comments on previous drafts of this paper.

Notes

1. Basic transcripts of all episodes are available online: www.friendscafe.org.
2. The symbol " ~ " in Extract 3 indicates "wobbly voice" (Hepburn 2004).
3. TCUs are "the building blocks out of which turns are fashioned" (Schegloff 2007, 3).

References

Attardo, S., and V. Raskin. 1991. Script theory revisited: Joke similarity and joke representation model. *Humor: International Journal of Humor Research* 4, no. 3–4: 293–347.

Billig, M. 2005. *Laughter and ridicule: Towards a social critique of humour.* London: Sage.

Bubel, C.M., and A. Spitz. 2006. "One of the last vestiges of gender bias": The characterization of women through the telling of dirty jokes in "Ally McBeal". *Humor: International Journal of Humor Research* 19, no. 1: 71–104.

Coates, J. 2007. Talk in a play frame: More on intimacy and laughter. *Journal of Pragmatics* 39: 29–49.

Drew, P. 1984. Speakers' reportings in invitation sequences. In *Structures of social action: Studies in conversation analysis*, ed. J.M. Atkinson and J.C. Heritage, 129–51. Cambridge: Cambridge University Press.

Edwards, D. 2005. Moaning, whinging and laughing: The subjective side of complaints. *Discourse Studies* 7, no. 1: 5–29.

Garfinkel, H. 1967. *Studies in ethnomethodology.* Englewood Cliffs, NJ: Prentice-Hall.

Glenn, P. 2003. *Laughter in interaction.* Cambridge: Cambridge University Press.

Haakana, M. 2001. Laughter as a patient's resource: Dealing with delicate aspects of medical interaction. *Text* 21, no. 1/2: 187–219.

Heritage, J. 1984. A change-of-state token and aspects of its sequential placement. In *Structures of social action: Studies in conversation analysis*, ed. J.M. Atkinson and J. Heritage, 299–345. Cambridge: Cambridge University Press.

———. 2005. Conversation analysis and institutional talk. In *Handbook of Language and Social Interaction*, ed. K.L. Fitch and R.E. Sanders. Mahwah NJ: Lawrence Erlbaum.

Hepburn, A. 2004. Crying: Notes on description transcription and interaction. *Research on Language and Social Interaction* 37, no. 3: 251–90.

Jefferson, G. 1984. On the organization of laughter in talk about troubles. In *Structures of social action: Studies in conversation analysis*, ed. J.M. Atkinson and J. Heritage, 346–69. Cambridge: Cambridge University Press.

———. 2004. Glossary of transcript symbols with an introduction. In *Conversation analysis: Studies from the first generation*, ed. G. Lerner. Amsterdam: John Benjamins.

Littlewood, J., and M. Pickering. 1998. Heard the one about the white middle-class heterosexual father-in-law? In *Because I tell a joke or two: Comedy politics and social difference*, ed. S. Wagg, 244–72. London: Routledge.

McHoul, A.W. 1987. An initial investigation in the usability of fictional conversation for doing conversation analysis. *Semiotica* 67, no. 1–2: 83–104.

Mills, B. 2005. *Television sitcom.* London: British Film Institute.

Mulkay, M. 1988. *On humour: Its nature and its place in modern society.* Cambridge: Polity Press.

Norrick, N.R. 1993. *Conversational joking: Humour in everyday talk.* Bloomington: Indiana University Press.

Osvaldsson, K. 2004. On laughter and disagreement in multiparty assessment talk. *Text* 24, no. 4: 517–45.

Pomerantz, A. 1984. Agreeing and disagreeing with assessments: Some features of preferred/dispreferred turn shapes. In *Structures of social action: Studies in conversation analysis*, ed. J.M. Atkinson and J. Heritage, 57–101. Cambridge: Cambridge University Press.

Robinson, J.D. 2004. The sequential organization of "explicit" apologies in naturally occurring English. *Research on Language and Social Interaction* 37, no. 3: 291–330.

Rockler, N.R. 2006. Friends, Judaism and the Holiday Armadillo: Mapping a rhetoric of post-identity politics. *Communication Theory* 16, no. 4: 453–73.

Sacks, H. 1992. *Lectures on conversation.* Vols 1 and 2., ed. G. Jefferson. Oxford: Blackwell.

Sacks, H., E.A. Schegloff, and G. Jefferson. 1974. A simplest systematics for the organization of turn-taking for conversation. *Language* 50, no. 4: 696–735.

Schegloff, E.A. 1968. Sequencing in conversational openings. *American Anthropologist* 70: 1075–95.

——— 2007. *Sequence organization in interaction: A primer in conversation analysis.* Cambridge: Cambridge University Press.

Apprentices to cool capitalism

Jim McGuigan

This article looks at the television series, *The Apprentice*, concentrating on the 2005 American edition and the 2007 British edition. *The Apprentice* is a game show that puts young business managers in competition with one another over several weeks. Every week someone is "fired". The reward for the eventual winner is an executive job with Donald Trump in the USA or Alan Sugar in the United Kingdom in the respective national series. It is a popular entertainment programme that also evokes key ideological assumptions about how to be successful in business. This is inscribed in the way the competition is organised between teams and individuals, the weekly tasks set for the teams and the rewards for each week's winning team. The article is part of a larger project on "cool capitalism" and aims to illustrate its ideological features through close analysis of the discursive operations of *The Apprentice*.

Introduction

The Apprentice, an American series with versions elsewhere, including a British franchise and a Chinese copy, *Winner*, is an emblematic television programme of the 2000s. This article aims to produce a critical analysis of the discourse of the third series of the American *Apprentice*, shown on US television in 2005 and in Britain in 2006. Reference will also be made to the 2007 British series and points of comparison drawn between the two versions, particularly concerning how class is signified in both countries but differently so.

The case study presented in this article is part of a larger project on "cool capitalism" (McGuigan 2006, 2009). At a time when the power of capitalism globally has never been so great and so extensive, its hegemony is little challenged. The public face of capitalism, however, has changed from its earlier, and some might argue its original, form in Protestant asceticism (Baehr and Wells 2002) to a much more hedonistic and "cool" appearance. Cool capitalism is largely defined by the incorporation of signs of disaffection and resistance into capitalism itself, thereby contributing to the reproduction of the system and reducing opposition to it. This is a vital feature of capitalism's hegemonic dominance now. It is a truism to say that hegemony has always to be won against counter-forces: its ideological principles constantly affirmed in the face of opposition, however weak. A programme like *The Apprentice*, then, performs an ideological role in projecting the values of free-market business in a seductive manner that disarms criticism.

A fully satisfactory analysis of media products should be multi-dimensional, taking account of various moments of production and consumption in the circulation of texts (Kellner 1997). It has become an established assumption that texts are consumed actively and, therefore, audience agency has a privileged position in media analysis. However, this may result in a virtual dissolution of the text, in effect, denying any textual determinacy whatsoever. This article seeks to recover a measure of textual determinacy in the social circulation of cultural meaning. It does not offer an entirely rounded analysis that would involve enquiry into production as well as audience research. Rather, it focuses specifically and more modestly on the text itself, obviously conditioned by the particular circumstances of production and open to differential interpretation by viewers.

The rules of the game

In looking at any television programme, it is necessary to locate it in relation to genre, identifying general features that it shares with other texts in the flow of television and also registering its distinctive and quite possibly peculiar characteristics. Like mass-popular cinema, the television institution must categorise its programmes in a manner instantly intelligible to audiences. This is especially important for television since it is such a voracious medium, producing huge volumes of output, much of which quickly becomes as dated as news. One-off programmes are not favoured by the commercial imperatives of the industry; the series form and, better still, the serial are widely considered crucial to the pragmatics of both production and consumption. *The Apprentice* is an occasional series/serial in that it has limited seasons of several episodes, each of which tells a discrete story – the completion of that week's task and ejection of a loser – whilst also serving as an instalment in a longer story unfolding over a season.

Like a great many television programmes today, the genre category of *The Apprentice* is hybrid, drawing most particularly upon game-show conventions and the conventions of "reality TV". The "reality" of *The Apprentice*, as in the reality effect of any such programme, is contrived – in this case, manifestly so since it is an artificially constructed game for which there are definite rules to be observed – and not purporting to be "a slice of life" in the raw. However, in addition to representation of the game – task-setting, team organisation, frantic activity and the resultant reward of winners and firing of a loser every week – the viewer is given some access to spaces and conversations "behind the scenes", particularly the suite in Trump Tower where the candidates retreat to rest and recuperate from the rigours of the game, although the game continues to be played there in subtle ways on camera during moments of relaxation.

As in all social situations, there are both formal and informal rules, the game's regulations and the less formal conventions of conduct that are not only deemed appropriate to the game but also to life in general. The whole person is, in some sense, on the line, each individual's private emotions and back story subjected potentially to voyeuristic scrutiny. Such information is either willingly proffered or concealed from view by the game players. They present themselves in specific and individuating ways: self-made, highly educated, spouse and parent, single-mother, "metrosexual", and so forth. Their self-definitions are projected, confirmed and put into question by the game. They are exposed to the other candidates, their judges and to the viewing public, although not in this particular reality game show a voting public as in, most notably, *Big Brother*, which is more expressly a popularity contest. The participants represent models of conduct, to be approved or disapproved according to extant ideological criteria of "the American dream", which involves the prospect of individual ascent to the top irrespective of social background, and correct – "enterprising" – business practice under neoliberal conditions. It is no accident that these shows owe at least part of their origin to social–psychological "experiments". The situation is, in effect, laboratorial.

The programme is formally a competition between carefully selected "candidates" – 18 in 2005 culled from a million applicants – to work with the great Donald Trump, the ultimate reward being to serve as his apprentice with the prospect of becoming as rich and famous as him. It is a long and arduous job interview. Although essentially an individualistic competition – there can be only one winner in the end – the game requires collaboration, formally and informally, between members of two contending teams seeking to complete a task more successfully than the other team, which usually, although not always, involves making more money. The essential balance between competition and collaboration, which includes occasional performances of team leadership – "stepping up to the plate" – in addition to mere membership (after all, the show is about business management), is a delicate process that some candidates, of necessity according to the rules of the game, are better at feeling for and satisfying than others.

There has to be a winner – that is, the fittest survivor of a gruelling ordeal; so there must be losers, one in each episode, condemned by the fatal "You're fired!" The stakes are high, the prize glittering and the cost of failure quite possibly very severe since candidates have usually given up their jobs in order to strive for the top job, to be the apprentice to Trump in the USA (Martha Stewart, on release from imprisonment for insider-trading, substituted for Trump in the fourth series) and Alan Sugar in Britain.

The Apprentice is educative in Gramsci's sense of mundane political education for the masses as well as *cadres* (Hoare and Nowell-Smith 1971), albeit accomplished through the mechanisms of sporting entertainment. The candidates are learning: and so are the audience supposed to be. This may be fun, but it is serious fun. In the American version and third series considered here, Trump literally teaches a lesson every week in the time-honoured tradition of entrepreneurial didacticism, testified by innumerable management advice books, the words of which appear on screen: 'Perseverance'[1] in the first week, followed in subsequent weeks by 'Respect Comes From Winning', 'Never Settle', 'Instinct', 'Play Golf' (Trump's favourite game, at which he considers himself to be rather good), 'Go Big Or Go Home', 'Sell Your Ideas', 'Let Nothing Get In Your Way', 'Pulling All-Nighters', and so forth. Each invocation is followed up with a little speech from Trump and, where possible, a practical demonstration of the lesson in that episode. Kendra's lone all-nighter in the episode to design a brochure for a Pontiac car was probably the turning point in the whole game, the nodal moment in the narrative when it became likely that she would win the 2005 competition.

It is important to notice the differential times of transmission and production. The programme's weekly episodes create the illusion of concise reports of the previous week's pro-televisual events, an ongoing reality. However, it is evident from the programme text itself that the whole series is shot and edited before transmission. This can be inferred by the ordinary viewer from, for instance, the weather and the times of dawn and dusk. This matters because, although each episode tells a story, the series as a whole tells an over-arching narrative: in effect, a meta-narrative, a grand story about stories.

The late Jean-François Lyotard, of course, would never have seen *The Apprentice*. Had he witnessed the instructive story it tells about the hegemony of cool capitalism in the 2000s, however, Lyotard (1984) [1979]) might even have revised his claim that meta-narrative no longer elicits credulity. This is not merely a comment on the serial/series structure of a television show but on the way in which *The Apprentice* represents in condensed form the grandest narrative of all today: capitalism rules without serious questioning, and that is "cool" since any conceivable question, however awkward, can be answered by business and logged into the greater scheme of things in a credible manner.

In studying genre, it is vital to note typical iconography, *mise-en-scène* and the characterisation of participants as players in the game in addition to selectively edited narrative and tempo. Certain settings and their contents are repeated throughout a series of *The Apprentice*: aerial shots of the Manhattan skyline with its skyscrapers, especially Trump Tower; the darkened boardroom with faces lit up, where Trump makes his judgements; admiring crowds when Trump occasionally issues his instructions to the contending teams on the street, supplemented most spectacularly by the applauding audience at the *denouement* in a theatre in the final episode; the various locales for each week's task, such as fast-food joints, department stores, offices, industrial plants, design studios, shops, leisure centres; luxury venues for the weekly reward to a winning team (restaurants, yachts and the like); and so on. There are bright mornings and dark nights; city lights; highways and byways. Everything happens at speed under tight time constraints, accompanied by popular music and the opening of each episode announced by "Money, Money, Money". This is a pressure-cooker environment.

The candidates are introduced at the beginning; their characters, educational and occupational backgrounds are sketched in and subsequently developed in action, their survival skills put to the test at every turn of events. They are a cross-section of young Americans: some hailing from ivy-league colleges; some from the wrong side of the tracks; men and women; whites and blacks; Northerners and Southerners; Western and Eastern; urban and rural. Social distinctions and typical identities are recognisable features of American culture and society, "the melting pot", familiar in more-or-less detail throughout the whole world, schooled in Americana through Hollywood movies, television shows and a rocking soundscape.

The third series

The opening episode of the third series establishes the format. Trump swoops into Manhattan in his personal helicopter and is whisked off to Trump Tower by stretch limo. He poses the programme's enticing question with the words printed on screen: 'What if you could have it all?' The Stars and Stripes flutters; Trump issues his paean to New York's "energy". "I'm looking for someone who can handle the pressure. I'm looking for someone who's a creative thinker. I'm looking for THE APPRENTICE". The candidates also fly in. There are 18 of them, all of whom are introduced deftly in this opening episode by their own words and moving portraits, by which time you might already decide who you will love and who you will hate. They are more-or-less pushy young Americans, mostly from the business world. They have to appreciate that in the ordeal they are about to face, 'It's nothing personal. It's just business'.

But, personality does matter. For example, guitar-playing Danny – nominated as a 'Marketing Technology Firm Owner' – is instantly presented as a problematic personality: "the other candidates wouldn't see me as a CEO". When he and the others gather together out of view and earshot of "Mr Trump", he puts himself forward as "the CMO – chief morale officer" and recommends a slogan to his team, "Unbelievable!" After all, he is a self-styled "out-of-a-box kind of a guy" in "a leisure suit", who makes up a ditty for his team, "Team Magna". Danny is like a throwback to 1960s hippydom, which immediately divides opinion among the contenders and elicits scepticism from Trump. His attempt to drum up custom by singing and playing guitar outside Burger King is a dismal failure but, in spite of the clownishness, he is not the one to be fired as a result of his team's failure in the first task. The loser is preppy Todd, the project manager, who plans badly and does not get stuck into customer service. After all, Danny is amusing, albeit an extreme and over-the-top avatar of cool capitalism, destined to be toppled before long in any case.

In the first episode, the candidates are divided into two teams, according to whether they are college-educated or only high school-educated – in Trump's words, "Book Smarts" versus "Street Smarts" – exemplifying the way in which class appears but is transcoded typically in what is supposed to be a classless society. The teams name themselves. The high-schoolers call themselves "Net Worth" because their combined earnings are three times that of the college-educated, straight away undercutting the educational advantages and disadvantages that might otherwise be associated with class. Even if they have never read a book, the Street Smarts know what counts, how to make money. The college-educated graduates call themselves "Magna", from "*Magna cum Laude*" on their college diplomas. The enigma of this particular series has to do with the value of a university education compared with "street" knowledge. Net Worth starts off well in the series but is later overhauled by Magna, and the eventual winner of the whole game turns out to be a university graduate from "a good school", in the American sense. So, education counts for something – Trump himself is a college graduate – but a mixture of both book and street learning is probably best. Tana, who came second, dropped out of college and had been something of a front-runner earlier in the game but slipped up when she lost her tact for leadership in the final task.

The sixth episode is especially significant since the college-educated beat the "Street Smart" at their own game and demonstrated that "cool" is all very well and, indeed, necessary so long as it maintains a business focus and does not get drawn too much into artiness. After all, it is a question of balancing college knowledge with street wisdom, culture with commerce. It is worth recounting the narrative of episode six in order to see how the discourse of *The Apprentice* achieves such a balance and, at a deeper level, resolves ideological tensions that erupt on the edge of the programme. This episode is about advertising Sony PlayStation's *Grand Turismo 4* video game. Trump outlines the task facing Magna and Net Worth this week:

> Nowadays, there's a new form of urban advertising. It's called graffiti. I'm not thrilled with graffiti but some of it is truly amazing. What you're going to be doing is creating a billboard using graffiti for PlayStation's newest product.

The teams will have to hire an artist to design the billboard for a wall in Harlem.

Some members of Net Worth go off to try out the game while Tara, project manager for the task, speaks directly to camera:

> I was project manager for this task because I understand Harlem. I wanted to tie the ad to that community. The city is a metaphor for the new game, the transition from the mean streets to like the new, more revitalised city.

Tara is black and "street wise". In the first episode she was nominated as a 'Senior Government Manager'; so she is the only candidate of the 18 who works in the public sector. This may have something to do with her community awareness and regeneration rhetoric. Another member of Net Worth, John voices doubts about linking a video game to what he calls "social consciousness". However, this task, like all tasks in the game, is commercially-driven. Concerned to display her marketing nous as well as "street cred", Tara sums up the target demographic: "urban, hip, 18–34 males". Alex, the "metrosexual" and smart-arsed project manager for Magna, talks about the artistic "concept" of the project that must conform to "the Sony message".

On arrival in Harlem we see "the mean streets" decorated with graffiti. In turn, the teams meet artists in Marcus Garvey Park where Magna recruit Lady Pink – whose creative aspirations run to "What does the person who's going to buy the GT4 want?" – while Net Worth sign up Ernie, a black artist who "can execute our vision [of] the mean streets of New York" (Tara). Tara wants to show "some respect to the people here because this neighbourhood is undergoing a major renaissance, as you can see ... grittiness ... the underlying theme, that's how things work". Craig, another black member of the team, warns her about keeping an eye on "your client, your customer". Alex of Magna, on the other hand, is worried about the social inappropriateness of his team members for this "street" task. So, he conducts "market research" by interviewing some young black men in the street (Trump's lesson for that week was 'Shut Up and Listen'). Informed by the research, Alex comes to the conclusion that "bling, bling, it is ... piles of cash raining down".

As presented in the programme, the narrative of the contest is very clear indeed, edited precisely to make the point. Quite simply it is this: Tara, better qualified with "street cred", allows the discourse of "cool" art to obscure the commercial goal of the task; whereas Alex, sensible to his deficiencies in terms of local knowledge, asks the people and discovers that they are more interested in money than outlaw art with the slogan "tear it up". Although Net Worth's graffiti billboard is better artistically, it is judged to be less effective in selling the product. Alex wins and Tara is fired. As Trump says: "This was a marketing task and you didn't get it".

This example – in some ways similarly to the problem of Danny – illustrates a significant feature of cool capitalism. Signs of cultural difference and even rebellion are embraced and incorporated by business, but not to the detriment of business, which some might otherwise and insouciantly assume to be so. The bottom line remains the bottom line, however "funky" the consumerist façade. The winners of the sixth episode, Magna, are rewarded by a "legendary" advertising photographer shooting their portraits in downtown Manhattan. As Alex remarks, this "taste of Mr Trump's lifestyle" has taken them from the mean streets of Harlem to "the top of the world".

All the candidates crave the great man's approval and they are always deeply impressed by the reward he gives for winning a task. In episode 11, the teams have to invent and sell a new Domino's pizza. The reward for Magna Corp's winning "Manga" pizza is breakfast in Trump's apartment at the top of the tower block. Kendra, the eventual winner, enthuses: "Trump's pad was bling, bling. Trump must have been a rapper in a former life because I've never seen so much gold trim in my entire life". The place is covered in gold leaf. Trump is especially proud of his extremely long and gold-painted dining table, which goes nicely with his bleached-blond quiff of hair. The table is so big that it had to be hoisted up the side of the skyscraper and passed into the apartment through an opened plate-glass window. "We needed to erect a special crane to lift it up". This is truly the high life in the eyes of the surviving candidates, dazzled by the ostentatious shine of it all.

The final episode, when the winner was eventually revealed, was transmitted live in the USA. This turns out to be, it is tempting to observe, a cross between the Nuremburg Rally and a Moscow show trial. Everyone already anticipates the probable winner, Book-Smart Kendra, who handled her reconstituted team of troublesome losers better than Tana handled hers on the final task. But, this is theatre. It is relevant here to recall the spectacular *denouement* to the previous season of *The Apprentice*, the second series. The final two candidates, Jenna and Kelly, the eventual winner – wind up in the boardroom to be grilled by Trump. Following a period of stern questioning, Trump asks them to leave the room so that he can consult with his advisors, right-hand man George and left-hand woman Carolyn. He remains undecided, then turns to address the camera: "I want your opinion. What do you think, right now?" Thanks to the magic of television, the boardroom, which is supposed to be several storeys up in the sky, suddenly swivels around and appears on the stage of a theatre in front of a large invited audience, applauding wildly on cue, adoring of Trump. Leni Riefenstal could not have stage-managed the event better and filmed it to more startling, although cheap, effect. This is Trump's stage and he will call upon his trusted employees in the audience to help him reach the final solution.

That stunt is not repeated in the third series. It is announced straight away that the venue is the arts centre at New York University. The audience is present from the beginning for the show trial of Kendra and Tana. They are interrogated in the presence of the gathered losers, who criticise and praise as is their wont. Kendra, as was fated, inevitably wins. Although she was quiet at the beginning of the contest, her record has been exemplary: three straight wins as a project leader and obtaining the successful cooperation of her reconstituted team in completing the final task. The journey has been Herculean and this young highly-educated woman with a keen and qualifying sense of cool culture and feel for the game is revealed as the natural winner, or so it seems, at the end of a seamless process in which Book-Smart and Street-Smart skills have been combined felicitously.

The British version

The British version of *The Apprentice* is presented by Sir Alan Sugar, who is by British standards a reasonably large entrepreneur but certainly not in the same league as Trump. Unlike Trump, Sugar's headquarters, for instance, are not actually in a downtown office block so have to be mocked up for television and represented in a City of London office building like Trump Tower in New York. His company's headquarters are out in East London. Although knighted (the candidates are always careful to call him "*Sir* Alan"), Sugar is from "a humble background". The winners of the first two series were a young black man of modest origins, working in the public sector, and a young white woman from a poor, socially-disorganised background. At the beginning of the third series that was televised in spring 2007, Sugar insists, presumably with the preceding results in mind, that he is not socially biased, in order perhaps to reassure fair play for those among the 16 candidates from a more privileged background than himself, most notably the private-school and Oxbridge-educated: "I don't care where you come from, whether you started in a council flat or born with a silver spoon. All I'm looking for is somebody who is drop-dead shrewd". On this occasion, he will – perhaps inevitably – chose someone from a comparatively privileged background with a public – that is, private – school and Oxbridge education. He announces his dislike of "schmoozers, bullshitters or liars" whatever their origins. Sugar is instantly recognisable in Britain as the very type of an East-End barrow boy made good. He is also evidently of Jewish extraction and known to support the ostensibly socialist New Labour Government, traits that may in the past – but hardly now – have been construed as representing outsiderness in the British economic and power elite. In the 2007 series, Sugar managed to square the circle and select a winner who actually shared quite a similar background to himself but complicated by social mobility over a number of generations, although this was not at all made explicit in the programme nor was it commented upon in the news media.

According to conventional yet dubious wisdom, fine distinctions of class difference are said to be more pronounced in British culture than in the "classless" USA. Nowadays, however, increasingly like America, class is not supposed to matter in Britain and reverse class prejudice is often decried as equally discriminating compared to the old top-down kind. The British are still sensitive to signs of class, however tortuously so, but quite possibly no more so than Americans. Still, social class is more markedly on the surface, so to speak, in the British version than it is in the North American version of *The Apprentice*. Also, questions of "race" and ethnicity are addressed with some sensitivity and they have become of greater prominence than in the past of British culture and society, similarly to the American preoccupation with "identity".

The persona of Sugar himself is especially notable, satirised brilliantly in Comic Relief's *Celebrity Apprentice* parody in March 2007, just before the commencement of that year's season. Similarly to the American prototype, Sugar also likes to fly about in a helicopter and boast of his own entrepreneurial achievements, although he is somewhat less ostentatious and brash than Trump. His speech is much more vulgar than that of Trump, illustrating the comparative permissiveness of British television's language code in comparison with the restrictions of American network television. He swears and enunciates what are generally regarded as rude yet witty similes to put down under-performing candidates. Generally, the tone of the British version is much more ironic and, indeed, tongue-in-cheek than the American original. There is an autopsy programme, *You're Fired!*, on BBC2 immediately following each weekly episode shown on BBC1, which invites that week's loser to face a studio audience, the members of which get to vote "hired" or "fired", to reverse or confirm, in their opinion, Sugar's decision, and before three invited "expert" guests commenting on that week's proceedings. Mostly, discussion is about the character of contestants and who is doing well and who badly. As with all successful reality shows on British television, there is constant coverage of the current show in the tabloid press – although generally, during the course of a season, the back story is kept firmly under wraps, necessitated by the delay between production and transmission. That the previous year's winner, however, Michelle Dewberry, had left Sugar's employment pregnant after only six months in the apprentice's job was a major talking point in spring 2007. Dewberry said that the position she had been given was unrewarding and that she could make more money as a freelancer, although she also insisted that she was still on good terms with "Sir Alan".

Here, I shall comment on just one episode from the third series, which is particularly germane to the argument concerning apprenticeship to cool capitalism. It is from week eight of the season and was first televised on 16 May 2007. In this episode, the two teams, Eclipse (originally the male team but now with one female member, Jadine) and Stealth (originally female and now exclusively so again), are given the task of branding and advertising a new pair of trainers ("sneakers" in the USA). Sugar greets them in Piccadilly Circus, "the most famous advertising arena in the world" where "brands fight for position". "Sir Alan" makes it clear what he wants: "an advert that sells kit. I do not want an advert that wins the Montreux award for advertising tossers". Tre, a marketing and design consultant who mixes what appear to be "fundamentalist" Islamic views, especially regarding the representation of women, with Sugar's own kind of arrogance, sardonic wit and vulgarity, is Eclipse's project manager for this task. Ghasal, also Asian but with a Scottish accent in contrast to Tre's cockney and very close to being fired, is given the chance to redeem herself as project manager for Stealth. The teams are advised that "the world doesn't need another trainer" so they had better come up with a really good "big idea". Tre instantly hits upon the winning formula for his team:

> All the street culture has been taken over by the big brands, yeh? So, what we're doing is we're reclaiming the streets. We're taking it back to the streets. We're giving them a [*sic*] underground alternative to the mass-produced representation of their culture.

The Eclipse team has already been out cool-hunting on the street, speaking with "the crucial youth market". They decide to name their trainer "Street". This strategy is supposed to be non-conformist and rebellious yet, in the trainer business, *pace* Nike, it is scarcely novel. It is, to all intents and purposes, thoroughly conformist, adopting signs of rebellion to accomplish the exact opposite: integration into the all-consuming culture of cool capitalism.

Stealth, unsurprisingly, also know that "cool" image matters but they are in trouble as a team with an inexperienced project manager, Ghasal, lacking street wisdom in spite of her youthfulness, and constant bickering between the posh Katie and the Irish Kristina (these characteristics of the two women are accentuated repeatedly in the programme). They call their trainer "Jam", which some wag says might sell well to the Women's Institute, and try unsuccessfully, in Sugar's judgement, to link its "solefulness" to music.

On the other hand, Eclipse have trouble hiring actors who can "bump 'n' grind" convincingly on their video. However, it transpires that Simon Ambrose, from the select and expensive London suburb of Hampstead Garden, is a song-and-dance man who can get down on the street. Tre is sceptical: "There's a fine line between good dancers and totally shite, bollocks dancers", referring to his mate, Simon. On this one, however, Tre eventually has to give in and acknowledge his earlier remark that Simon is "a very talented boy". Simon composes and delivers, in a passably "street" hip-hop accent, a rap to accompany street moves on the video that convinces the team, and eventually Sugar too. Not bad for a white, middle-class and Cambridge graduate from Hampstead Garden Suburb, incidentally, from where Sacha Baron Cohen, a graduate of Cambridge too – Ali G and the world-famous Borat – also hails. Simon's rap goes as follows:

> Street is not about corporate branding, high-street fashions and rip-off pricing. It's not about country walks and village fetes. Street is about giving back, revolutionising the system, taking back control. It's about knowing yourself, knowing your style and representing your culture, representing the street. Reclaim the street!

Having borrowed the slogan "reclaim the street" from the anti-capitalist movement, Simon is called urgently away from the recording studio where he has been laying down the track to break-dance on the video, which he also does with some *panache*. One of Sugar's advisors, Margaret, describes Simon as "a rapping acrobat": if that is what "Sir Alan" wants, so be it. Since Simon was eventually appointed "the Apprentice" she was not proven wrong.

There is a problem, however, with the "Street" campaign. The team agrees, at Tre's behest, that a percentage of the take should be donated to "street youth centres". There is some disagreement over whether this should be from the £39.99 price or from the profit. In the end, the billboard advert says, "10% of every sale will go to street youth centres". Tre himself had wanted the 10% to come from the more nebulous profit. In the brightly-lit boardroom setting of the British version, Sugar thinks likewise:

> You're forcing the consumer to pay four pounds. They won't like that. I can promise you, they won't like that. What it should have been is that you are gonna give away some of your profits. That way the customer doesn't know what you're actually gonna give away but the sentiment is there.

Still, however, Eclipse win and the team members are rewarded by learning to make cocktails at the Ritz – very street. And Ghasal is fired after a fierce denunciation from Sugar of her talents and negative forecast of her long-term prospects. Katie now also looks to be on borrowed time, although she later made a comeback and was selected by Sugar for the final round in the competition. That she declined the offer confirmed his suspicion that Katie all along was after the publicity but not the job. In her words, she was then cast by Sugar as "the pantomime villain".

Conclusion

When analysing a television programme such as *The Apprentice*, it is important not to just impose the abstract terms of a linguistic model on the object in question. There is a texture to the text that is not reducible to words; images and sounds also matter and have a logic of their own that complicates the meaning of the words. It is difficult to convey such a highly textured discourse solely in words, and still images are inadequate in conveying the flow of the text. Moreover, the present article treats a complex cultural phenomenon in relation to ideology: namely what I have called "cool capitalism", the articulation of which within the programme is illustrated most sharply with reference to the episode on graffiti-advertising in the 2005 season of the US *The Apprentice* and the episode on designing and marketing a pair of trainers in the 2007 season of the British version. The articulation of cool capitalism in the two series is not reducible to these two episodes but best exemplified by them for illustrating the focal point of the argument.

  While this particular article is dedicated to an enquiry into the ideological legitimisation of capitalism today, especially its appropriation of "cool" signs and symbols, thereby potentially neutralising opposition, there is no guarantee that the lessons taught are effectively learnt by the viewing public. The appeal of the programme is first and foremost that of a game show and a kind of soap-operatic play of character and story over several weeks. That *The Apprentice* is imbued with market values and seeks to validate the absolute worth of capitalist business whatever the human cost – most obviously the arduous testing of candidates in the show in order to reveal the fittest, although much more serious than that in terms of the complex structures of exploitation perpetuated by global capitalism – is no secret. It can be enjoyed without succumbing to the message. I enjoy it, admittedly from an anthropological point of view, not simply as a matter of educative entertainment. There is little doubt, however, that such popular fare contributes to the articulation of a capitalist reality as the only reality, and it does so by appealing to people, in a sense, on their own ground: hence there are significant differences between national versions of the show. From a business point of view, it is probably a joke, an artificial and trivialising entertainment that bears no real relation to a real reality. That evaluation rather misses the point of the evocation of a fantasy business world that marks out the boundaries of the social world itself.

Note

1. In this article, when quoting printed words on screen I use a single quotation mark (') convention; when reporting speech I use the convention of a double quotation mark (").

Notes on contributor

Jim McGuigan is Professor of Cultural Analysis in the Department of Social Sciences at Loughborough University, UK. He has published several books, including *Cultural Populism* (1992, Routledge), *Culture and the Public Sphere* (1996, Routledge) and *Modernity and Postmodern*

Culture (2nd edition; 2006, Open University Press). His latest book, *Cool Capitalism*, will be published by Pluto in 2009.

References

Baehr, P., and G. Wells, eds. and trans. 2002. *The Protestant ethic and the "spirit" of capitalism and other writings of Max Weber*. London: Penguin.

Hoare, Q., and G. Nowell Smith, eds. and trans. 1971. *Selections from the prison notebooks of Antonio Gramsci*. London: Lawrence & Wishart.

Kellner, D. 1997. Critical theory and cultural studies – The missed articulation. In *Cultural methodologies*, ed. J. McGuigan, 12–41. London: Sage.

Lyotard, J.-F. 1984 [1979]. *The postmodern condition – A report on knowledge*. Trans. G. Bennington and B. Massumi. Manchester: Manchester University Press.

McGuigan, J. 2006. The politics of cultural studies and cool capitalism. *Cultural Politics* 2, no. 2: 137–58.

———. 2009. *Cool capitalism*, forthcoming. London: Pluto.

"Our England": discourses of "race" and class in party election leaflets

John E. Richardson

This article examines two election leaflets distributed in Bradford, UK as part of the May 2006 local election campaigns of the Labour Party and the British National Party. Drawing on critical discourse analysis, the article shows that prejudicial ethnicist discourse is not solely the purview of marginal far-right political parties, but is incorporated by mainstream British political communications. Specifically, I argue the two leaflets share similar ideological assumptions and arguments: first, of English exceptionalism; second, a representation of migrants as "things" that we have a *right* and a *need* to manage in the interests of "Our" nation; and third, the complete elision of class identity and conflict when examining who benefits from the exploitation of migrant workers.

Introduction

Issues relating to immigration, asylum, and cultural, religious and "racial" differences currently have a prominence in British domestic politics to a degree not seen for over 20 years. In their recent study of "Britishness" during the last three general elections, Billig et al. (2005) demonstrate that, during the 1997 election, immigration and racial or cultural difference barely featured as a reporting theme: mentioned in only 1% of coded election news reports, they were placed 14th behind more "bread and butter" issues. Since then, they have steadily crept up the league table of presupposedly salient electoral issues: 12th in the 2001 General Election with 2.5% of coded reports (above employment and defence); then up to *fourth* most frequently reported during the 2005 election with 7% of coded reports, more prominent than crime, the National Health Service, or even education. Illegality and the threat assumedly posed by foreigners to "our security, prosperity and way of life" are issues very much back on the landscape of British political life.

At the centre of this campaigning is Britain's largest far-right party, the British National Party (BNP), although the nature of their involvement is a matter of dispute. Some academics – for example, Schuster and Solomos (2004, 280) – have argued that it was the success of the BNP in local elections that "drove New Labour into a stance of aggressive defence in relation to migration, and specifically asylum". While this certainly represents the defence of New Labour, Sivanandan argues that: "The BNP did not give rise to racism. Racism gave rise to the BNP" (cited in Bourne 2006). Thus, it was "widely noted that when the BNP were elected in Tower Hamlets in 1993 immigration had been an important issue nationally. Similarly, the issues of immigration and asylum have been a national concern in the last few years" (Rhodes 2005, 9), and so the BNP have gained local councillors in places such as Burnley, Blackburn, Halifax, Stoke and now Bradford. The BNP are capitalising on the current legitimacy granted to anti-immigration discourse via their popularisation by mainstream politicians and journalists and, in doing so, have secured minor electoral successes.

Following Hopkins (2001, 185), I assume that:

> if we wish to understand the relationship between national identification and discriminatory action we should investigate the construction, dissemination and reception of different versions of the nation's boundaries (i.e. who belongs), the contents of identity (i.e. what it means to belong) and the nation's relations with others.

For illustrative purposes this article will examine two party election leaflets – one from the BNP and one from the Labour Party – distributed in the Royds ward of Bradford during the 2006 local elections.[1]

Critical discourse analysis

The relationships between text and context form a principal focus of discourse analysis. Discourse analysts emphasise, first, that discourse should be studied as language in use – we are interested in "*what* and *how* language communicates when it is used *purposefully* in particular instances and *contexts*" (Cameron 2001, 13; emphases added). We assume that language is a social practice that, like all practices, is dialectically related to the context of its use. Second, discourse analysts assume that language exists in a dialogue with society: that "language simultaneously *reflects* reality ('the way things are') and *constructs* (*construes*) it to be a certain way" (Gee 1999, 82). Thus, language represents and contributes to the production and *re*production of social reality.

Critical discourse analysis (CDA) represents a growing body of work within this general approach to language use. Critical discourse analysts argue that if we accept the second general principle of discourse analysis – that language use contributes to the (re)production of social life – then, logically, discourse must play a part in producing and reproducing social inequalities. In response, "CDA sees itself as politically involved research with an emancipatory requirement: it seeks to have an effect on social practice and social relationships" (Titscher et al. 2000, 147), particularly relationships of disempowerment, dominance, prejudice and/or discrimination. To examine how discourse relates to systems of social inequality, analysis needs to be focused at three levels: on texts; on the discursive practices of production and consumption; and on the wider socio-cultural practices, which discourse helps (re)produce. Taking each in turn: first, the analysis of texts involves looking at the form, content and function of the text, starting with "analysis of vocabulary and semantics, the grammar of sentences and smaller units, and [...] analysis of textual organisation above the sentence" (Fairclough 1995, 57). Recently, multi-modal analysts of the grammar of visual design (Kress and van Leeuwen 2006) have introduced a new dimension to this level of analysis. They point out that all texts are multi-modal, in the sense that "spoken language is always accompanied by paralinguistic means of communication such as [...] gesture and posture, and that written language is always also a visual arrangement of marks on a page" (Anthonissen 2003, 299). A multi-modal approach requires analysts to examine the communicative potential of *visual* elements – that is, the way "they can create moods and attitudes, convey ideas, create flow across the composition, in the same way that there are linguistic devices for doing the same in texts" (Machin 2007, xi).

Second, one needs to consider the discursive practices of the communicative event, which usually involves an examination of "various aspects of the processes of text production and text consumption. Some of these have a more institutional character whereas others are discourse processes in a narrower sense" (Fairclough 1995, 58). A key assumption of this level of analysis is that textual meaning cannot be divorced from the context of social and discursive practices (Fairclough and Wodak 1997). An author or producer may encode meaning into a text (choosing one view over another, choosing an image rather than another, etc.), but the text also acts on the producer, shaping the way that information is collected and presented due to the conventions of the text-genre under construction (Richardson 2007). At the point of consumption, a text is decoded by readers who have (differentiated) perspectives, agendas and background knowledge of both the text-genre under examination and the motives of its author(s) or producer(s). Party election leaflets are a very specific genre of public discourse that unfortunately very few academic articles have taken as an object of study. Political leaflets are far more likely to be listed along with other forms of political communications than be subject to detailed analysis in themselves. The dearth of academic analysis is all the more odd given the centrality of such media to contemporary party campaigning. One study of the 2005 British general election, in which respondents recorded every contact they received from political parties, found that on average "respondents received 11.51 total contacts" and "the vast majority of these were leaflets and letters" (Fisher 2005, 2). To be precise, of the 3592 contacts with political parties recorded by respondents, 3459 (96.3%) were leaflets or letters (Fisher 2005).

Finally, Fairclough (1995, 57) suggests that a fully-rounded critical discourse analysis should involve an analysis of the text's "sociocultural practice", or "the social and cultural goings-on which the communicative event is part of". This level of analysis

> may be at different levels of abstraction from the particular event: it may involve its more immediate situational context, the wider context of institutional practices the event is embedded within, or the yet wider frame of the society and the culture. (Fairclough 1995, 62)

Political leaflets – like any discourse – "are situated in, shaped by and constructive of circumstances that are more than and different to language" (Anthonissen 2003, 297). With this in mind, this article now moves to a discussion of immigration legislation and the recent campaign activities of the BNP.

Social contexts, social practices

New Labour and anti-immigrant discourse

Since the introduction of the anti-Semitic 1905 Aliens Act, British political discourse has, almost ubiquitously, constructed immigration as a *problem* that politicians need to *solve*. However, as Lewis and Neal (2005, 437) argue, it is following the 1962 Commonwealth Immigration Act that successive Labour and Conservative governments' *shared* strategy of "ever increasing immigration controls and legislation has worked to fuel populist and political demands for ever tighter restriction", preventing the entry of groups of (predominantly *non-White*) people "who previously had automatic rights to citizenship" (Schuster and Solomos 2002, 45). Clearly, Britain in the 2000s is a different place from Britain in the 1960s; however, a number of key continuities can be observed. As Dummett has argued, since the 1960s British political discourse has assumed two things: first that "the British masses are racist"; and second

> that in comparison with the masses all political leaders and 'Establishment' people are [...] liberal and must bend their efforts to restraining or quietening down any popular signs of racism, brushing it under the carpet where they don't succeed in cleaning it away. (Dummett 1973, 244)

These assumptions open up an argumentative space in which it is possible for elites "to adopt positions defending racist measures while criticising certain people for acting in a more racist manner than them, or for using intemperate language" (Dummett 1973, 244).

Since New Labour were voted into power in 1997, they have introduced a great range of policies on immigration and asylum, including three major pieces of legislation, "a range of secondary legislation and a raft of new initiatives" (Schuster and Solomos 2004, 274).[2] The primary focus of these policies is on keeping those they view as "undesirable migrants" out of the country, particularly asylum-seekers. The 2002 Nationality, Immigration and Asylum Act represented a partial shift in immigration discourse, creating a pathway for those deemed to be "useful migrants" – in short, migrants useful for the production of surplus value. However, the Act also enacted a shift "away from affirmations of British multiculture towards a (re)embracing of older notions of assimilation within a newer, de-racialised language of social cohesion" (Lewis and Neil 2005, 437).

As stated in the introduction, the Labour Party "assumed that fear of migration, and asylum seekers in particular, was responsible for an increase in support for the BNP and that therefore the government had to be seen to be addressing these concerns" (Schuster and Solomos 2004, 278). Unfortunately they "addressed" these racist preoccupations by *confirming* rather than *contesting* them. Indeed, the then Home Secretary Jack Straw is on the record in 2001 arguing for "a limit on the number of applicants, *however genuine*" (*Observer*, 20 May 2001).[3] This limit, he explained, would be set by "the ability of the country to take people and public acceptability". Similarly, in 2003, the then Home Secretary David Blunkett argued that New Labour's third major piece of immigration and asylum legislation was necessary because "people who are not engaged in politics need to know we've got a grip, that we know what we are doing and understand their fears" (*Observer*, 12 December 2003).[4] New Labour opted to play the BNP on their own ground, attempting to appear tough on immigration in order to be "acceptable" in the eyes of anti-immigrant sections of the electorate, seemingly unaware (or *indifferent*) to the fact that the far-right and their supporters have been yelling "too many" and "this country's full" since the 1950s and even earlier.

Bradford, the BNP and localised campaigning

Rhodes (2005, 6) has observed:

> It was the victory of the BNP in Tower Hamlets in 1993 that served to reinvigorate academic interest in the far right in Britain [...] Since 2000, the BNP have made further and much more striking inroads, gaining local councillors in places such as Burnley, Blackburn [and others].

Like Burnley and Blackburn, Bradford can be described as "a traditional textile and manufacturing base that is in long-term decline, a low wage economy, relatively high levels of socio-economic deprivation and high crime rates" (Copsey 2004, 131). Despite these similarities the racist mobilizations the BNP was able to make focused on markedly different issues. In Oldham they centred on fears regarding increasing numbers of racially motivated attacks on Whites [...] while in Burnley they have been based around issues of "positive discrimination" and a belief that the council has spent disproportionate funds in the predominantly "Asian" area of the town. (Rhodes 2005, 7)

Indeed, this localisation of both policy and political rhetoric is such a dominant approach that the BNP have recently attempted to build "an alliance with radical anti-abortion activists in an attempt to reach out to Catholics and secure their votes in future elections" (*Observer*, 4 March 2007)[5] – this despite being a staunchly *unionist* party. Of course, such localisation should come as no surprise given the "yearning for homely living embodied in nationalist discourse", often involving "an idealisation of the nation [articulated] through the idealisation of locality" (Hage 2003, 34).

In Bradford, the principal thrust of BNP campaigning has been centred on what the party call the *Islamification* of the city, with "racial" and cultural difference used to explain an array of social, economic and political issues. Such a standpoint has been a regular feature of far-right agitation in Bradford, at least since Ray Honeyford, a local head teacher, wrote a series of articles in the *Salisbury Review* attacking multicultural education policies. More recently – and echoing Rhodes' (2005) research into BNP campaign strategy in Burnley – Bradfordian:

support for the BNP has come from the more affluent sections of the town. Supporters of the party have been drawn not just from the decrepit working-class areas [...] but from the leafy semi-rural suburbs and the streets adjacent to quaint village greens. (Rhodes 2005, 13)

In the 2006 local elections, the BNP's Peter Wade was placed second, receiving 28.6% of the vote in the Eccleshill ward in the North East of Bradford, less than a mile from the expansive Woodhall Hills Golf Club; Ian Dawson also placed second in the Keighley West ward, with 33% of the vote; whilst Paul Cromie was voted in as BNP Councillor for Queensbury, on the moor-edge in the far west of the city, with 38.5% of the vote. In all of these areas, the BNP presented themselves as reasonable, local people who care for the community: they are the only people willing to tell the truth about the problems of the country; and they have the courage to offer the "common sense" answers that "Our country" needs.

Analysis

The analysis of these two leaflets is presented across two axes: first, a brief multi-modal analysis of the visual dimensions of the texts, concentrating predominantly on the use of photographs, page layout and typography; and second, the linguistic content of the leaflets, paying particular attention to referential strategies and argumentative structure. However, "national identities encompass material practices as well as discursive practices" (Wodak 2006, 106) and so, throughout, the discussion of these leaflets will relate their ideological narratives to various economic and political practices.

British National Party

The BNP's leaflet is highly visual, using 14 photographs, a range of typefaces, and a clever use of layout[6]. The "10 Point Plan" for example (Figure 1), seems, purposively laid out: the

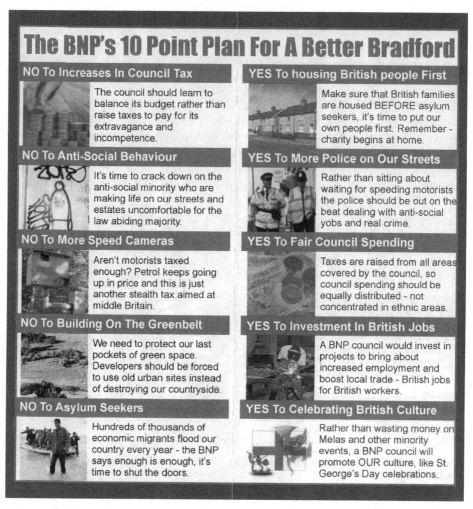

Figure 1. BNP 10-point plan.

party's views for and against an issue, in the left and right columns, often match up (e.g. anti-social behaviour – more police; No to asylum seekers – celebrate "OUR culture"), or else cascade diagonally down into each other (e.g. homes for British families – improving "life on our streets"; more police – no more speed cameras; "British jobs for British workers" – no more "economic migrants"). It is interesting to note that this layout supports Kress and van Leeuwen's (2006) domains of given and new, with the problems they argue against on the left presumed to exist and their proposed policies on the right. Further, this interplay, across and between the policies outlined in the "10 Point Plan" indexes the integrated, mono-causal political ideology of the far-right. The policies *appear* linked because they *are* all, implicitly or explicitly, linked to a single cause: the presence of undesirable people in Britain. Such social groups are referred to explicitly as "asylum seekers" and "economic migrants";[7] implicitly as ethnics (cf. those who live "in ethnic areas") and minorities (cf. "minority events"); and are grammatically included as part of "Them", a nebulous entity who appear to be housed before "our own people" and whose events currently "waste money" to the detriment of promoting "OUR culture". Wells and Watson (2005, 271) have also noted such vague conflation, within "a discourse that collapses together the identities of British ethnic minorities and reveals the plasticity of the concept of 'asylum-seekers' which, in fact, is used interchangeably with 'refugees', 'Muslims', and often, simply 'they'". While the BNP would not state it quite this baldly in their election materials, the overriding sense is that the problems "We" experience in tax, housing, crime, employment and culture could be solved with the *forced removal* of "Them" – the undesirable "ethnic" contingent spoiling Bradford.

When the reader first opens the folded leaflet, the facing page (Figure 2) introduces the key issue of the election for the BNP, and indeed for reactionary politics in general: Islam. The use of the photograph of the blown-up bus in Tavistock Square, 7 July 2005, is typical of the way that relationships between nation and "matters of race, faith or culture have been formulated in response to an immediate 'crisis'" (Condor 2006, 8). The image, and the event that it pictures, are clearly coupled to Islam through the use of the text overlaying the photograph. The choice of this specific typeface – scratchy, jagged and irregular, as if it has been gouged out of the picture – evokes the artwork of the "slasher movie", and underlines the BNP's view of Muslims as violent, chaotic and out of control. This representation of Muslims is also reflected in the second photograph on this panel: a rather standard "Muslim horde"-type photograph, whose placards contextualise the photograph as a demonstration and spell out their grievance in graphic violent terms. The presumed threat they pose is also communicated through the way the subjects fill the frame – a composition that suggests both a large crowd and that "they" (the many) cannot be contained, spilling over the borders of photographs and countries.

It is interesting, however, that the angle of interaction places the viewer in an elevated position above the crowd. Conventionally, this is taken to connote a power relation: to give the viewer a sense of power over the group in the image by depicting them as literally subordinate to the viewer (Machin 2007). At the heart of the photograph, therefore, is a tension, or perhaps a contradiction, typical of far-right ideology. The image emphasises the threat that an "ethnic other" poses to "Us" by virtue of their number and their threatening views, whilst simultaneously positioning the viewer in an *empowered* role and in a position to *manage* this "ethnic other". The remaining two photographs, of the candidate Cromie, are strikingly different to the representation of Muslims. In both images the person pictured is an individual, who engages with the viewer through the use of direct gaze; the angle of interaction is horizontal; the image is a mid-close shot – close enough to suggest intimacy but distant enough to maintain a sense of detachment; and she is depicted in a rural setting, in contrast to the (inner?) cities in the other two photographs. The meaning potential of these choices foregrounds the sense that Cromie is an approachable individual, friendly and serene, and on "the same level" as the us, the viewer – the antithesis of the meaning potential of Muslims in the other images.

In the middle of one side of the leaflet is a panel that, due to the way that the leaflet is folded, would ordinarily be read last. Examining its linguistic contents, it certainly seems designed with this function in mind: it provides summaries of the BNP's "common sense" approach; it reiterates a central organising theme of their campaign (that the interests of "ethnics" are being put above "British people"); and it builds to a closing *anaphora* in "it's time for …", "it's time for …", "it's time to …", "it's time to …".[8] The middle paragraph is significant in relation to the party's political arguments:

Figure 2. BNP treatment of Islam.

Political correctness is now dictating how we should think, even nursery rhymes like Baa Baa Black Sheep are being banned in schools as they might "offend members of ethnic minority communities" – what utter madness

Here we have a standpoint about the "utter madness" of political correctness supported by a symptomatic argument (see Atkin and Richardson 2007) about nursery rhymes. The rhetorical force of the paragraph is heightened through several discursive features. First, the argument about nursery rhymes is introduced by a scalar implicature: that *even* nursery rhymes, childish, innocuous and fun, are not beyond the meddling attention of "Political correctness" – here nominalised in order to conceal who exactly the BNP believe has been issuing such diktats. Second, nursery rhymes is pluralised, with "Baa baa black sheep" cited as one example of the kind of rhyme being banned, suggesting this is the first of several or many. Third, the reason why these rhymes are being banned is presented in speech marks, a device that indicates it is the view of some third party. This construction distances the BNP from the truth claim while simultaneously providing a straw man for the party to argue against. Similar stories about banning "Baa baa black sheep" have been circulating since the 1980s. Along with banning black bin-bags, such stories act as a trope for the excesses of liberal politics, and have been repeatedly and demonstrably falsified (see Searle 1989). However, in this case, the origins of the story do have some basis in fact. In March 2006, the BBC reported that two nurseries in Oxfordshire were teaching children new versions of the rhyme involving differently coloured sheep.[9] But the charity running the nurseries stressed that this was for educational reasons, and nothing to do with "race": "They sing happy, sad, bouncing, hopping, pink, blue, black and white sheep etc and they also exchange boy and girl at the end of the rhyme. This encourages the children to extend their vocabulary and use up some energy." Viewing everything through their distorted racialised lens, the BNP re-textualised this story as an(other) example of foolish pandering to ethnic minorities, when it was no such thing. Indeed, even the central premise – that the "black" in "Baa baa black sheep" was to be proscribed – is false.

Labour Party

As with the BNP's text, there are repeated banal references to the nation (Billig 1995) in Labour's leaflet (see Figure 3). Banal nationalism involves "the unquestioned, common-sense presumption that the proper unit for social concern and moral accountability involves the nation or state" (Condor 2006, 6). This imagining of the nation entails a corresponding imagining of foreignness beyond the border of the country – a foreignness that, in this leaflet, dovetails uncomfortably with the passive objects of "Our" pity characteristic of inferential racism. However, the Labour leaflet is about "England" not "Britain", and it sports the flag of St George, not the Union Jack. This complicates the nationalism articulated, as English nationalism is particularly ambivalent and is disconnected from the banal nationalism of conventional politics. After all, although England is constitutionally a country, it does not exist as a specific political unit; nor does it exist in relation to citizenship. So, the ideological question arises: why is England being used?

Labour have attempted to achieve two somewhat incompatible argumentative acts with their leaflet. First, they are clearly seeking the support of those in the electorate who are tempted to vote BNP – voters who do not see the benefits of immigration and therefore want it restricted or stopped entirely. Second, they must counter the perception that Labour's restrictions on immigration are motivated by bigotry, thereby avoiding the accusation of xenophobia or even racism. Labour's resolution to this double bind rests on

The Labour Party wishes you a Happy St George's Day

Figure 3.   The pictorial element in the Labour leaflet.

an attempt to appropriate the language, and iconography, of English patriotism from the political far-right, whilst simultaneously attempting to nullify its partiality.

In a similar way to a campaign strategy in the 1997 general election, the Labour Party has used St George and his cross as symbols of national pride (Billig et al. 2005). This, in itself, implies that Labour supposed the BNP-leaning voters identified themselves as *being* English, otherwise the emphasis would be misplaced. However, it is interesting to note that the BNP does not actually lay any rhetorical claim to the English flag. In fact, as stated, the BNP is a unionist party and uses the Union Jack in its logo and across its campaign literature. The image of the flag itself is arresting, depicting a fluttering flag tied at the hoist to an invisible halyard and pole. Movement of the flag, implied by both the faux-blurring around its edge and the way that it curves and loops back from left to right, evokes a dynamism, liveliness and vitality that would have been lacking had an image of a flat, rectangular flag been selected. The curvation of the flag also acts to soften the straight and perpendicular lines of the cross. This lends the image a greater sense of "gentle", "natural" and "organic" cultural associations over "harsh", "technical" and "masculine" values that tend to be associated with angularity (see Machin 2007, 99–100).

Using the English flag, the Cross of St George, in such a prominent way – a sign whose far-right connotations have only recently started to shift – could be especially problematic for the leaflet's argumentative goals. And so, in the text that accompanies the image, the party attempts to shape the audience's understanding of the various meanings of the flag in a way that is beneficial to their rhetorical aims. They do this by listing "three great English characteristics": "fairness, decency and tolerance". These are the values that they wish the flag to metonymically symbolise so that when we – the assumedly English reader – see the flag, we feel proud. Written without a determiner – that is, "*the* three great English characteristics" – implies that these characteristics are three taken from a potentially longer list, a device that intensifies the valorisation. The BNP, the leaflet argues, have misunderstood what Englishness means, refusing to support black footballers playing for England, and condemning the *noblesse oblige* of those who gave to the Tsunami relief effort. Hence by destabilising, and then strategically *redefining*, what it means to be patriotically English, Labour attempt to claim what is typically a more right-wing preoccupation, in order to position themselves as the natural party of the *English* nation. But it is interesting to note that rejection of the BNP's intolerance is articulated in conjunction with a rather chauvinistic idea of English exceptionalism. Specifically, the sense is that "fairness, decency and tolerance" are *distinctively* English characteristics. Simply put, if tolerance is thought of as a "great English characteristic", this implies that the people of other nations are less tolerant. So, while the BNP rhetorically position those they call "the ethnics" as an *inferior*, or *unworthy* social group, in their leaflet Labour rhetorically position the English as being a *superior* social group.

There is also a more fundamental contradiction at the heart of New Labour's valorisation of "English tolerance" due to its reliance on a "double process of de-racialization and re-racialization" (Fortier 2005, 562). Lewis and Neal (2005, 441) explain that within New Labour's multicultural nation there is, on the one hand, "a requirement for others' 'sameness' (assimilation) but on the other hand, in order to make the claim for multicultural tolerance there is a need to re-inscribe, within clear limits, the (acceptable) other as other". The Labour leaflet claims that the originally non-English migrant can unproblematically become English – the rhetorical upshot of claiming "Englishness is created by its people", some of whom are "recent newcomers". If this is the case, and "newcomers" add inevitably to the mix that is "Englishness", who or what is it, exactly, that the English are tolerating? To whom are "We" being decent and fair if newcomers (automatically?) become part of "Us"? The narrative presupposed in this portion of the leaflet, in which England is the product of "successive 'waves' of foreign invasion and settlement", draws on a form of conventionalised historiography wherein the nation is *augmented* with *additions* to the existing *ethnos* (Condor 2006, 17). By such an account, Englishness is a kind of "stew that grew" (see Hage 1998) – but one with an "Anglo" stock at its base.

With this in mind it is useful to examine how "newcomers" are constructed in this Labour leaflet: they are to be "welcomed" but in a "managed" way, with the understanding that "they" are here to help "us" "afford our future pensions and public services" and avoid "economic ruin". In contrast to the "zero-immigration" approach, which dominated the Conservative governments of the 1990s, (New) Labour's objective for "managed migration policies is the facilitation of movement across frontiers in a way that would produce the maximum benefit *for British interests*" (Flynn 2005, 464–465). However, a more detailed examination of such policies reveals "a system which is dominated by *business* interests" and which "structures political discourse around the high ground of a scientific and technological progressivism in which the interests of business entrepreneurs are privileged" (Flynn 2005, 465). Of course, capitalism hardly encourages benevolent employment practices, but the regulatory framework for employing newly-identified "migrant workers", introduced by New Labour, clears the ground for their untrammelled exploitation.[10]

The leaflet therefore supports a specific form of *ethnic managerialism*, in which the human rights of newcomers are subservient to the demands of the market. In fact, this ethnic managerialism, discharged in the interests of the business class, is at *the heart* of the Labour leaflet – arguing, on the one hand, that it is "illegitimate to discriminate against someone on the grounds of race" while, on the other, it is "perfectly legitimate to discriminate against someone on the grounds of nationality or economic utility" (Billig et al. 2005, 31).[11] The leaflet presents an immigration policy directed by the narrow financial interests of bosses and shareholders in support of a material reality in which a migrant class of worker is denied many basic rights. In essence, Labour has sedimented "a system of stratified rights – or civic stratification – which can serve as both a statement of rights and an apparatus of surveillance and control" (Morris 2002, 410). In Labour's discourse, migrants are reduced to a resource ripe for economic exploitation – workers whose value to profiteering bosses is evidenced in the leaflet through the use of some very specific and accurate-looking statistical facts.

Conclusions

The aim of the present article has been to discuss the relationships between national identity and racist exclusion in contemporary British politics. More specifically, I have sought to examine the expression of nationalist and racist sentiment in political leaflets, and illustrate the utility of discourse analysis – drawing upon the multi-modal analysis of Kress, van Leeuwen and Machin alongside a socio-diagnostic approach to CDA – in taking apart such texts. Two leaflets, one printed by the BNP and the other by New Labour, were used as indicative cases intended to illustrate that prejudicial ethnicist discourse is not solely the purview of marginal political parties, but is incorporated into the mainstream of British political communications.

In the words of Schuster and Solomos (2004, 283):

> Migrants, especially asylum seekers and undocumented migrants, have become the targets of racist campaigns [...] It has become evident that rather than questioning and challenging some of the press and public misperceptions around this question New Labour has, if anything, stoked them.

There is evidence of this stoking here in this leaflet. In terms of immigration law, "Englishness" has absolutely no status at all and immigrants who adopt the nationality of the land into which they migrate do not become "English citizens". Therefore, the rhetorical mobilisation of Englishness in the Labour leaflet must rest upon reclaiming a more classically ethnic, rather than civic, version of nationalism. Such an English nationalism must be based on *cultural* assumptions about what Englishness is; it cannot be based on the legal discourse of English citizenship, for there is no such discourse open to the Labour party. Once immigration is talked about in terms of English nationalism (whether openly or implicitly) it cannot be phrased purely in legal, non-ethnic, civic terms: it has to use the discourse of cultural privilege. And, while Labour's rhetoric is by no means as vitriolic or explicitly prejudiced as that of the BNP, it nevertheless draws on similar ideas: first, of English exceptionalism; second, a representation of migrants as things that we have a *right* and a *need* to manage in the interests of "Our" nation; and third, the complete elision of class identity and conflict when examining who really benefits from the exploitation of migrant workers. In articulating this national "We", other potentially salient categories of individual and social identity – class, for instance – are elided, or at least are only employed in support of the posited primordial national identity. Significant class differences – between boss and worker, or between working, middle and upper classes – need to be eradicated in order to achieve "Our" rhetorical national unification.

Epilogue

Linda Cromie (BNP) was not successful in the 2006 local elections in the Royds ward of Bradford. However, she stood again and, on 3 May 2007, was elected as councillor for the neighbouring Queensbury ward – joining her BNP husband on the Bradford council.

Acknowledgements

The author is grateful to Joseph Burridge, Michael Billig and the attendees of both Loughborough Culture and Media Analysis Research Group and Lancaster Language, Ideology, Politics for their comments on earlier drafts of this article.

Notes

1. Many thanks to Dominic Wring for providing me with these leaflets.
2. These included the 1999 Immigration and Asylum Act; 2000 Race Relations (Amendment) Act; 2002 Nationality, Immigration and Asylum Act; 2004 Asylum and Immigration Act; the "New Vision for Refugees"; and others. At time of writing, the Labour government has recently launched a Green Paper – *The Path to Citizenship: Next Steps in Reforming the Immigration System* (2008) – that solidifies their attack on the poorest of Britain's immigrants.
3. Available from http://www.guardian.co.uk/politics/2001/may/20/uk.election20018 (accessed 27 June 2008).
4. Available from http://www.guardian.co.uk/politics/2003/dec/14/immigrationandpublicservices. immigration (accessed 27 June 2008).
5. Available from http://www.guardian.co.uk/uk/2007/mar/04/thefarright.otherparties (accessed 27 June 2008).
6. Due to copyright restrictions, this article reproduces only parts of the analysed leaflets. The full leaflets are included in the version available online at: http://www.freewebs.com/johnrichardson/academicarticles.htm.
7. This referential strategy is used under the heading "NO to Asylum Seekers", implying that the BNP consider these two distinct legally-defined social groups to be one and the same.
8. The third and final paragraph of this panel reads: "The old parties only care about lining their pockets and looking after the interests of different minorities. It's time for a change, it's time for commonsense, it's time to put the British people first – it's time to vote British National Party, the commonsense party.
9. Nursery opts for rainbow sheep, *BBC Online*, 7 March 2006. http://news.bbc.co.uk/1/hi/education/4782856.stm (accessed 24 May 2007).
10. Flynn demonstrates that the possibility "that migrant workers could access the range of rights provided for in a range of international human rights instruments, such as International Labour Office regulations and the United Nations Migrant Workers Convention, or the Convention on the Rights of the Child, or the European Convention on Human Rights is *emphatically precluded by*" the Home Office White Paper *Secure Borders, Safe Haven* (Flynn 2005, 478; emphasis added).
11. This acceptable face of discrimination was also implicit in a speech Tony Blair gave on 22 April 2005 in Dover – a highly symbolic town to English nationalist border discourses. He declared: "In financial services – a sector which now employs 300,000 and brings billions of pounds into our economy. Migrants play a key role in some of the most skilled jobs in the world. We will not turn

our back on *these or other migrants contributing so much to our economy and our society"* (emphasis added; see http://politics.guardian.co.uk/labour/story/0,9061,1466504,00.html, accessed 23 May 2007).

References

Anthonissen, C. 2003. Interaction between visual and verbal communication: Changing patterns in the printed media. In *Critical discourse analysis: Theory and interdisciplinarity*, ed. G. Weiss and R. Wodak, 297–311. Houndmills: Palgrave.

Atkin, A., and J.E. Richardson. 2007. Arguing about Muslims: (Un)Reasonable argumentation in letters to the editor. *Text and Talk* 27, no. 1: 1–25.

Billig, M. 1995. *Banal nationalism*. London: Sage.

Billig, M., J. Downey, J.E. Richardson, D. Deacon, and P. Golding. 2005. *"Britishness" in the last three General Elections: From ethnic to civil nationalism*. A Report for the Commission for Racial Equality.

Bourne, J. 2006. Labour's love lost? http://www.irr.org.uk/2006/february/ha000021.html (accessed 24 May 2007).

Cameron, D. 2001. *Working with spoken discourse*. London: Sage.

Condor, S. 2006. Representing, resisting and reproducing ethnic nationalism: Official UK Labour Party representations of "multicultural Britain". Paper presented at the VIII International Conference on Social Representation, 30 August 2006, in Rome, Italy. http://www.psych.lancs.ac.uk/people/uploads/SusanCondor20060822T094425.pdf (accessed 15 May 2007).

Copsey, N. 2004. *Contemporary British fascism: The far right and the fight for political recognition*. Basingstoke: Palgrave.

Dummett, A. 1973. *A portrait of English racism*. London: Penguin.

Fairclough, N. 1995. *Media discourse*. London: Arnold.

Fairclough, N., and R. Wodak. 1997. Critical discourse analysis: An overview. In *Discourse studies: A multidisciplinary introduction*, ed. T.A.van Dijk, Vol. 2, 67–97. London: Sage.

Fisher, J. 2005. *General Election 2005: A voter's eye view*. Initial findings report. The New Politics Network and The Joseph Rowntree Reform Trust. http://www.jrrt.org.uk/Voter_Eye_View.pdf (accessed 27 June 2008).

Flynn, D. 2005. New borders, new management: The dilemmas of modern immigration policies. *Ethnic and Racial Studies* 28, no. 3: 463–90.

Fortier, A.-M. 2005. Pride politics and multiculturalist citizenship. *Ethnic and Racial Studies* 28, no. 3: 559–78.

Gee, J.P. 1999. *An introduction to discourse analysis: Theory and method*. London: Routledge.

Hage, G. 1998. *White nation: Fantasies of white supremacy in a multicultural society*. Annandale: Pluto Press.

———. 2003. *Against paranoid nationalism*. Annandale: Pluto Press.

Hopkins, N. 2001. National identity: Pride and prejudice? *British Journal of Social Psychology* 40: 183–6.

Kress, G., and T. van Leeuwen. 2006. *Reading images: The grammar of visual design*, 2nd edition. London: Routledge.

Lewis, G., and S. Neal. 2005. Introduction: Contemporary political contexts, changing terrains and revisited discourses. *Ethnic and Racial Studies* 28, no. 3: 423–44.

Machin, D. 2007. *Introduction to multimodal analysis*. London: Hodder Arnold.

Morris, L. 2002. Britain's asylum and immigration regime: The shifting contours of rights. *Journal of Ethnic and Migration Studies* 28, no. 3: 409–25.

Rhodes, J. 2005. The "local" politics of the British National Party. *SAGE Race Relations Abstracts* 31, no. 4: 5–20.

Richardson, J.E. 2007. *Analysing newspapers: An approach from critical discourse analysis*. Houndmills: Palgrave.

Searle, C. 1989. *Your daily dose: racism and the Sun*. London: Campaign for Press and Broadcasting Freedom.

Schuster, L., and J. Solomos. 2002. Rights and wrongs across European borders: Migrants, minorities and citizenship. *Citizenship Studies* 6, no. 1: 37–54.

———. 2004. Race, immigration and asylum: New Labour's agenda and its consequences. *Ethnicities* 4, no. 2: 267–87.

Titscher, S., M. Meyer, R. Wodak, and E. Vetter. 2000. *Methods of text and discourse analysis.* London: Sage.

Wells, K., and S. Watson. 2005. A politics of resentment: Shopkeepers in a London neighbourhood. *Ethnic and Racial Studies* 28, no. 2: 261–77.

Wodak, R. 2006. Discourse-analytic and socio-linguistic approaches to the study of nation(alism). In *The SAGE handbook of nations and nationalism*, ed. G. Delanty and K. Kumar, 104–17. London: Sage.

The ontology of a self-help book: a paradox of its own existence

Scott Cherry

The self-help book is celebrated as an iconic feature of popular culture. Indeed, as a non-fiction genre, the self-help book has become a global publishing success. However, the self-help book displays no recognition of its connection to a genre of writing, characterising itself as a singular, solitary text. This article engages a body of research and practice that has unproblematically assumed this normative, "self-sufficient" characterisation in its commentary of the self-help book. This article explores the self-help book as a textual form whose appearance as "self-contained" is deployed as part of a rhetorical strategy to invoke "reading". It shows that the self-help book displays in its discourse an anxiety around this characterisation. This is unpacked by examining the self-help book through a paradox: on the one hand, reading a self-help book is characterised as the single requirement for its readers to fulfil their quest for self-help; while, on the other, that invocation of reading is in itself insufficient for self-help.

Introduction

Smiles (1859, 1) first set out the project of self-help in his book of the same title, suggesting that "[h]elp from without is often enfeebling in its effects, but help from within invariably invigorates". A most apparent observation is that the term "self-help" attaches itself to phenomena recognisably "external" to the individual, most notably the publishing phenomenon of "self-help books". If the individual interacts with a reading object, where *it* bears the name "self-help", then following Smiles, this implies "help from without". But self-help, "help from within", has to preclude the self-help book; however, without the latter, self-help disappears. It suggests several questions: where is self-help to be located – in the self-help book or in the reader of the self-help book? How might we characterise the reading process and the way in which it constitutes the quest for self-help? Such is the purpose of this article.

The context of popular culture

The self-help book is recognised as an icon of popular culture; it is, in effect, popular culture itself. Starker (1986, 1988, 1990) has charted its prevalence across most spheres of cultural life – the home, the marketplace, recreation, relationships, hobbies, health and illness, bereavement, family, and so forth. We find these books in bookshops, libraries, supermarkets; we receive them as gifts, talk about them at work and read them at bedtime. Virtually every country that has a written language offers self-help books by native authors or translations from abroad; many self-help books go through multiple editions (Holgate 2005). Its cultural significance pivots on its appeal to a mass market. It acquires its "iconic" status in part due to its being able to apply to *any* individual who selects it. Thus, the self-help book has continued to appear on bestsellers lists for the past 70 years (see Hansen, McHoul, and Rapley 2003; McGee 2005).[1]

The popularity of the self-help book as a publishing category is reflected, even amplified, in its own social critique. A rising body of critique has problematised the popularity of self-help literature, focusing its attention on the deceptive "undertow" with which the genre is afflicted. The self-help book market, it argues, has deluded the reading public by creating in its members a co-dependency; rather than helping themselves, readers have become reliant on the self-help book for the satisfaction of their needs (Justman 2005; Salerno 2005; Tiede 2001). Interestingly, this critique has had a "popularising" effect on the self-help book market. This critical writing has tended to make self-help book authors reaffirm their practices, an effect of which, ironically, has been an even more explicit formulation of the self-help book genre. Thus, the self-help book, in spirit and deed, continues to prosper as a publishing phenomenon.

The self-help book on prescription

The use of self-help books emerged in a professional and medical context in the 1970s (Glasgow and Rosen 1978; Ruben 1979). Professionals have certainly recognised the appeal of "do-it-yourself" therapy from the commercial context of self-help books (Starker 1988). Therapists and psychologists have articulated their widespread use of self-help books as part of normative health care practice (Starker 1986, 1990). Although largely an American domain of practice, a number of healthcare initiatives in the United Kingdom have introduced the self-help book as a category of treatment in areas of psychological health (Frude 2004; Farrand 2005). The self-help book thus occupies an established place in the professional context, where its agency is displayed at all points of its application. We can chart it being prescribed by practitioners, spoken about in consultation as medical knowledge, evaluated as treatment and introduced to patients as a diagnosis. It has been endowed with the responsibilities of a medical apparatus – an operational, configured object whose "medicational" attributes define its application. Like the drug medications with which it is designed to compete, the self-help book is prescribed *as* a function of its status as a "self-sufficient" unit of medication. Reading "releases" its reason for prescription; and reading is the activation of treatment.

The self-help book as cultural discourse

The research literature has attended to the self-help book as a substantive cultural phenomenon (Hazledon 2003; Blackman 2004; Dolby 2005; McGee 2005). It has attended to the ways in which the self-help book operates under the auspices of the reader as simultaneously the "problem" of and "solution" to their life circumstances. It focuses on how the self-help book organises its discourse, and its readers, by endorsing hyper-individuality. Thus, self-help books disregard the context of social influence, and instead extol the importance of the responsibility of the reader to care for themselves, an ethical and moral commitment to their own stability. It is argued that the self-help book assumes the reader has a problem in relating to or treating himself/herself, and, being the location of certainty, diagnoses the pursuit of a programme "in which the reader must learn to *love* the self" (Hazledon 2003, 417; original emphasis). The reader is endowed with a certain kind of "personal wholeness" from which they have digressed, and to which they must return, if only they can attune themselves to those powers of mastery and self-sufficiency (Rimke 2000).

This research literature takes a critical stance towards individualism. It argues that the self-help book disregards any possibility that the reader has no "unique" self, represented in those practices that imply it and existing independently of cultural context (McGee 2005, 179). This corpus of work characterises the self-help book as symptomatic of an overarching set of psychological discourses that works to regulate and "control" the individual through the appearance of choice and autonomy. It adopts a broadly Foucauldian perspective to elucidate the status of the self-help book as an example of those techniques and procedures of the government of the private lives of citizens through the authority of psychological expertise. And it accomplishes this through the emergent cultural dominance of the "psy" complex in which it is situated (Rose 1990).

Opening an analytic approach

My approach to the analysis of the self-help book is informed by a general ethnomethodological appreciation of the displayed, practical and therefore analysable methods by which social phenomena are instantiated. More specifically, this approach draws on literary theory and criticism in considering the inscription/reception interplay of codes, conventions and other symbolic features of textual production and interpretation. This offers a methodology with which to develop an understanding of the self-help book by examining certain thematic and semiotic patterns as they operate in and as this textual form. This approach interrogates the self-sufficient characterisation of the self-help book, charting those procedures and devices used for its deployment and the rhetorical uses to which they are put. On the notion of readers, as an empirical phenomenon, we need also to identify the constitution of a readership. Therefore, this kind of transactional analysis engages the self-help book around those points at which readers are "encoded" and then "decoded" as part of the management of the reading process. By uncovering some of those normative features, we can spell out how the self-help book not only constructs its readership but how, and in what ways, it invokes that readership for the accomplishment of reading.

The research literature and professional practices have ostensibly endowed the self-help book with some variably-specified value that is "extracted" by a reader in the process of reading. It is treated as given that the status of the self-help book remains ontologically constant, displayed clearly in the medical context, where the self-help book is prescribed because *it* is able to change the status of its reader. It has taken the act of reading to be axiomatic, the passive reception of the self-help book's meaning. However, these assumed features – the "value" of the self-help book, the process of "reading", the status of "a reader", "problems" – emerge through a writing and reading contingency. And these are precisely the sites of action whose character remains concealed when one simply considers the status of the self-help book as "present" before the reader, and whose value resides "in" the text.

The self-help book has been approached, remarked on and considered as a manifestation of some wider, more significant phenomenon. One consequence of this position is that it dissolves the particularities of context into the generalities of "culture", "society", "structure", and so forth. The self-help book then becomes a passive "exemplar" of that which it represents, controlled by those forces exerted from overarching conditions. But, as a context of action, it begs "the question of just how, and for whom, culturally and historically recognizable formations take on their relevance to the moment at hand" (Suchman 2007, 16). To begin to understand that the self-help book occupies a place in the world as a constitutive context of practice, we need to "move away from a structuralist premise that prior conditions fully specify what it means to act within the prescripts that institutionalised society provides" (Suchman 2007, 16). Instead, we need to explore the self-help book as a site of practical activity, enacted through the contingencies of that context and with the relevance of "wider" cultural formations emerging from that practice.

Analysis

Prioritisation of the self-help book

The first contact a reader has with a self-help book will invariably be the "blurb" scattered across its front cover. This is part of the peritextual production of a self-help book, which serves up the content of the work: "offers" it to its readership (Genette 1997, 16). One form of this production is the orderly appearance of sales figures since the work was first published:

Over 3 Million Copies In Print.[2]

This is not a straightforward announcement of the volume of sales achieved by each title, a mere statement of fact; this has a clear illocutionary force. The inclusion of strong sales figures invokes a sense of achievement, recognition. A high volume of sales becomes a criterion of success of the self-help book, which neatly forms a self-exemplifying, recursive mechanism for its own justification: the self-help book is of value because millions of copies have been purchased; millions of copies have been purchased because the self-help book is of value. Sales status is also formulated as part of other, related modes of success, the rhetorical effect remaining the same – popularity as mass appeal figures as the measure of evaluation:

The International Bestseller.[3]

The international circulation of a title implies a transcendence of the boundaries of culture. This comments not so much on the homogenisation of different cultures as to the extent of variability to which the self-help books appeals. In other words, although it is received across complex population and cultural formations, in which the social contexts of its readership might well vary significantly, the self-help book continues to survive. It is against this variability of reception that a constant is brought into relief – a single, nameable object: *this* self-help book.

Here, a measure of success is "rank" in a competitive marketplace with other self-help books; "outselling" competing titles upgrades the status of this self-help book, indicating that its popularity functions through a discerning readership, being selected *in preference* to other self-help books. Note: "the" instead of "a" precedes the category bestseller; thus the self-help book is not simply *a* bestseller but *the* bestseller. That prefix, "the", assigns this self-help book a singular character, as in the best, only or most remarkable; in effect, it conceals the visibility of a self-help book genre. The would-be reader has no legitimate reason to search for other, alternative self-help books – the "best" is already under consideration. At any rate, this characterisation announces this self-help book as an authoritative treatment. It is a publishing phenomenon whose prevalence entitles it to be conceived in the singular, as incomparable.

What we see at this peritextual level is the summoning of the reader to venture beyond the threshold of the text into "the work", part of what we might provisionally call "hooking" the reader. Of course reading does not simply result from "crossing" this threshold; he/she may not have been "caught" by this hooking device. Thus, the self-help book as self-sufficient is a device ongoingly deployed, in various forms and guises, to satisfy the uptake of reading. In *S/Z*, Barthes (1974) shows how and when "codes" of meaning in a text organise the act of reading. For instance, a hermeneutic code refers to any element in a narrative that, although providing details, only reveals partial meaning and thus deliberately evades disclosure. These "suspended answers" and "snares" maintain the enigma of the text; they "keep it open" (Barthes 1974, 76) to the extent that the reader seeks its resolution through the work of reading. For instance:

> Life is difficult. This is one truth, one of the greatest truths. It is a great truth because once we truly see this truth, we transcend it. [. . .] Most of us do not fully see this truth that life is difficult. Instead, they moan more or less incessantly, noisily, or subtly, about the enormity of their problems, their burdens, and their difficulties as if life were generally easy, as if life *should* be easy. [. . .] Do we want to moan about them or solve them? (Peck 2006, 3; original emphasis)

Peck formulates a narrative as concerns some condition of the "natural" order of the world: that "life is difficult" points to a level of generality and speaks in the most unspecified, general terms possible. Specificity is not required here, for this truth is a generalised, overarching state. A related concern, with a similarly natural mechanism of operation, is the response of people to that world: that is, those who fail to "fully see that life is difficult" and undertake to "moan" about its difficulty. So we have, on the one hand, the stated character and prior existence of a world, and, on the other, those upon whom this world exerts its difficulties.

However, Peck's focus is not the problem of life, or, more generally, some quality of the world, but those interpretations of, and orientations to, that world. This separation assembles two points of location: the first is people, as a site for "modification"; and the second is the world that is self-regulated, a fixed point against which that modification can be judged. This is not so much *characterising* as *informing* the reader. The idea that moaning as a response to problems, to life, represents an endemic solution strategy, which characterises the way "most of us" engage life, is not meant to refer to those strategies of the reader. In other words, the "us" to which Pecks refers, as some majority population, is set up as part of the same "inherent" condition as the original "life is difficult" condition; it refers to a generic population whose moaning strategies have concealed the truth that life is difficult. To be sure, this is made especially clear when the population to whom the category "us" refers now gets modified, referred to as "they". And those people, now referred to as "they", identified as an "out-there" population, we can only assume will continue to be presented with problems and, failing to see them as an inherent part of life, continue to moan about them.

The formulation of Peck's question "Do we want to moan about them or solve them?" arises at a critical juncture. The category of reference has once again shifted, moving from "us", then "they", to "we"; the question is being addressed to a different, more specific population. This can be teased out further by considering a similar example:

> They go struggling, perhaps even whining, through their days with a sense of dull resentment at what they consider the "bad breaks" life has given them. In a sense there may be such a thing as "bad breaks" in this life, but there is also a spirit and method by which we can control and even determine those breaks. (Peale 1952, ix)

Peale elaborates this further with his deployment of two categories of plural pronoun, "they" and "we". This use of "they", like Peck, forms a generic audience merely indexed as a category of people against which a more specific "we" audience is currently being addressed. The addressed reader is thus part of a readership wishing to pursue that quest for improvement: those wishing to "control" and "determine" the "bad breaks", those who will seek the truth and transcend it by facing their problems. These people, to be sure, can be distinguished as such from that category of others "out-there" for whom the book does not apply, the generic "moaners". The "we", then, refers to those for whom the task of reading will be a beneficial enterprise, given that they have selected the book and are being addressed by virtue of that selection. Having formulated the enigma of the text – that life is difficult, that there are those who fail to overcome such difficulty, that there is a method of controlling that difficulty – there are "various subordinate and interpolated clauses [. . .] all of which precede the ultimate predicate (disclosure)" (Barthes 1974, 84).

The use of the plural pronoun "we", more than simply "making a clearing" for readers, is inviting them to undertake the process of reading so as to bring about the revelation of the text: that is, acquire those methods to determine the bad breaks, achieve self-help. Thus, "we" refers to a class of category-bound activities (Sacks 1992, vol. 1: 333–340). Readers are thus impelled to participate with the text: to be sure, a dialectics is being assembled between the self-help book and the extratextual "life" of the reader. If members of the "we" category – those whose membership has already been invoked as part of its formulation and contrast to the "they" category – find that they do not currently pursue those category-bound activities, then they "have a program laid out, which is to make it true for them" (Sacks 1992, vol. 1: 336). Quite how readers will "make it true for them" is, however, still largely unspecified, not least because there is still a level of generality around who is being addressed. It is unclear how (and if) the "we" category relates to *this* reader of the self-help book. But:

> [Y]ou face challenges and problems each and every day. You . . . may feel that what is happening to you simply is not fair. If a problem is important to you, then that's enough; that qualifies it as worthy. It's important, because *you* are important. (McGraw 1999, 11–12; original emphasis)

The general, third-person plural form has now disappeared; but so has the first-person plural form "we". Substituted is an individual, singular form, a specific person referred to as "you". This pronoun shift introduces the self-help book as a form of engagement to an individual reader as against categories of people to which any single reader belongs. However, this pronoun usage, in itself, does not specify its reader in any axiomatic fashion. The interpretative work carried out by readers as a general practice of reading – that is, to think in terms of identity and similarity – is implicitly being invoked; readers are being asked to make the connection between the encoded reader addressed and the "actual" person who is reading the book. And through this conjunction of the reader with the text (not to be mistaken with "the author" as such), readers' interpretive work must follow "*the intention of the text*" (Eco 1992, 25; original emphasis). McHoul (1982) has demonstrated how readers make sense of their routine interactions with texts by underscoring the readerly use of the documentary method of interpretation. Readers apply this method by "treating an actual appearance as 'the document of', as 'pointing to', as 'standing on behalf of' a presupposed underlying pattern" (Garfinkel 1967, 78).

Supposing that a reason for reading a self-help book is the reader's lack of knowledge concerning the nature of some "problem", particularly how to solve it, then it must only be vaguely specifiable prior to undertaking the action that is intended to bring about its solution. And there will be some "correspondence" here as the formulated narrative of the self-help book acts as a template for readers' understanding of their problems. As readers ongoingly search for meaning, any current remark can alter the sense of prior remarks, so that reading is not just cumulative and prospective but reassembles current material retrospectively. And with readers' interaction requiring a response as an individual (an "I"), their personal "problems" – that is, their exposure to, interpretation, and incorporation of their lives, however idiosyncratic – provide the frame from which this text is to be interpreted. The life of the reader becomes a resource at his/her disposal; specific problems of the reader become candidates of the general narrative of the self-help book.

More important, simply by the fact and manner of this form of engagement, readers' problems are explicable in the same terms as those general problems and difficulties of life. Thus the reader has identified herself/himself as being the addressee of the self-help book. This self-identification forms part of the assignment of responsibilities, issuing certain *reasons* for reading. Not being the cause of those problems of life but being able to determine their solution, reading is "accommodated" to fit the pattern-so-far; the reader is "choosing" to pursue the quest for self-help. Such is the documentary method: an interpretative device for binding retrospective/prospective, part/whole text configurations, and textual/extratextual relationalities (McHoul 1982).

Having over-determined the hermeneutic code, making readers a highly visible concern by recruiting them into the text and underscoring their importance, also affords authors certain rhetorical privileges. As Adorno (1994) discovered with his analysis of newspaper horoscopes, this code appeals to the easiest defence: narcissism. In seducing the reader, ostentatiously "playing up" to their ability to "determine" the course of their lives, self-help book authors command attention in as much as "vanity is nourished by so powerful instinctual sources that he who plays up to it gets away with almost anything" (Adorno, 1994, 53). One effect of this, for the self-help book, is that it imparts a snare with an increasingly firm hold over the reader:

> You are now accountable; you have always been accountable; you will always be accountable. That is how it is. (McGraw 1999, 56)

In accrediting the reader with a capacity for action, routinely practised as part of his/her life, McGraw is prefacing important leverage to secure the uptake of reading *by imposing obligations of reader agency*. The reader, if the code is interpreted thus, comes to see that not only does he/she have the ability to determine future action but that he/she has "always" exercised this capacity. An assumption is that every action the reader has made is an action for which he/she can be brought to account; it invokes agency to perform self-help. As an example of the reader-as-agent, which makes visible the effects of agency and the accountability therein, another set of authors propose the following:

> It may seem safer to keep things as they are – indeed the very thought of change may cause a temporary increase in anxiety! It is important to remember to confront the reality that although limitations in your lifestyle [. . .] may make your life more "comfortable", in the long term such restrictions are very disabling. (Silove and Manicavasagar 1997, 48)

Although undertaking to discard the book, to "keep things as they are", may indeed be a consideration, it is also an action, and as such demonstrates an active orientation *away* from self-help. It displays readers' accountability: abandoning the book occurs not because the reader is *unable* but because he/she *will* not help himself/herself. The consequences of not reading, whose "restrictions are disabling", emerge because the reader has *chosen* those conditions. There is a linear narrative here, with *only* two courses of action proposed: the first, already discouraged, and the second, reading, which is being encouraged. Reading is preferable, desirable; the self-help book has become a *requirement*. Furthermore:

> If you read this book thoughtfully, carefully absorbing its teachings ... you can experience an amazing improvement within yourself. (Peale 1952, x)

Peale's assurance that reading the self-help book will deliver what is required for the reader is indeed given, formulated as an extreme case (cf. Pomerantz 1986) – it will bring about an "amazing improvement". However, the requirement of reading is heavily qualified: attaining that amazing improvement is conditional upon fulfilling the "if" clause in the initial proposition. Nonetheless, provided a specific method of reading is fulfilled, the reader *ought* to expect this "amazing improvement".

Problematising reading

The reader is the focus of modification in as much as he/she is required to transform the capacity to interpret life differently, so as to determine the nature of their interaction with the world. This is the promise of the self-help book, fulfilled by reading. The site of this transformation is located as an attitude of mind; controlling how the reader relates to the world, to his/her benefit, involves a change in how he/she thinks about that world:

> But practice thinking confident thoughts, make it a dominant habit, and you will develop such a strong sense of capacity that regardless of what difficulties arise you will be able to overcome them. (Carnegie 1936, 23)

A considerable debt owed to reading a self-help book is the change of attitude it produces in the reader. An important phase of reading is to get the reader to adopt a way of thinking that responds to the world in the affirmative; it converts every "negative" into a "positive" (Woodstock 2007). The reader is asked, for instance, to repeat affirmations aloud, daily:

> I am a positive person.
> I enjoy challenges.
> I am an excellent mother/father/son etc.[4]

We are not concerned with the actual or "empirical" reader here: part of our traction on the self-help book concerns how it gets the reader to recognise and agree to the necessary competence postulated by the text for him/her to meet its promise (Eco 1992). Thus, affirmations, dictated by the reader, *as the author of them in their speaking*, are a display of positive thinking. There is significance to speaking these affirmations – the reader is *doing* something with the written text. Thus, although transforming thought patterns is indeed an action performed reflexively by the reader, and is necessary to achieve the quest for self-help, it is nevertheless treated as "inherently" problematic, flawed; it is not an action in the practical sense. Although reading has been prescribed as the requirement for improvement, its status as a mode of self-help is being reconfigured as part of the reading process:

[I]t is not sufficient to apply to the mind even such an important affirmation therapy [...] unless throughout the day you also base your actions and attitudes upon fundamental principles of happy living. (Peale 1952, 71)

Reading, like the change in thinking it has set forth, remains on the page of the self-help book, in the mind of the reader; it is of little *practical* use. At any rate, it is difficult to document how reading (or positive thinking) has an effect without, so to speak, authenticating it, having some reportable means by which the reader can *evidence* the change-as-a-result-of-reading. Thus, reading (and thinking) can only be considered in terms of actions: that is, how the reader can demonstrate – *show* – an improvement by pointing to it. This is anticipated by the way reading is organised around extratextual activities, the first of which being the practical instantiation of affirmations: that is, *saying* rather than just *reading* them. And so the reader is asked to perform questionnaires, exercises and other non-reading tasks:

Wear a rubber band loosely around your wrist. When you feel a panic attack starting, stretch the rubber band out and let it snap back on to the inside of your wrist. Often, the short, sharp sensation of pain will be enough to redirect your attention away from the beginning of panic symptoms. (Silove and Manicavasagar 1997, 85)

Wearing a rubber band, stretching it and feeling its impact on the wrist in controlling a panic attack are practical actions, located beyond reading and beyond the self-help book; importantly, unlike reading, these actions are reportable as evidences of self-help. The status accorded "reading" is becoming increasingly clear by the way the practical character of self-help is emphasised as the preferred route through the self-help book. The reader is guided along a predetermined path of progression as the self-help book displays its *ideal* effects by responding with specific remarks and eliciting those expectations that further reading will satisfy. One author says: "Try to reward yourself for coping with the panic attack by treating yourself to something you like".[5] The author foresees a template of the preferred reader, a person who is "able to deal interpretively with the expressions [of the self-help book] in the same way that the author deals generatively with them" (Eco 1979, 7). And in reaching the end of the self-help book, the reader is once again assured of what has been achieved:

You are now equipped to make a life strategy that allows you to begin changing your life, one step, one goal, one priority at a time. (McGraw 1999, 266)

What we can observe, in tandem with the prioritisation of action (doing) over reading (thinking), is a return, from the temporality of the reading experience of the self-help book, to the general, temporally unspecified and "continuous" unfolding of life. The reader is being re-oriented, placed back into a life beyond the self-help book from whence he/she came. Through the process of reading – which the self-help book has assumed has been carried out as prescribed, as noted by its explicit control over *how* the reader reads and interprets its text – the reader has undergone a transformation. The status of the self-help book has changed in terms of what it represents to the reader. Like Plato's famous ladder of knowledge, which the philosopher ascends in his search for truth, the reader of the self-help book, in searching for self-help by the effort of reading, advances the rungs of the ladder, passing from ignorance to knowledge. Reading "consumes" the self-help book: it simultaneously deprives the text of value by empowering the reader with knowledge.

> The final rung, the level of insight that stands (or, more properly, on which the reader stands) because it is the last, and is, of course, the rejection of written artifacts, a rejection that, far from contradicting what has preceded, corresponds exactly to what the reader, in his repeated abandoning of successive stages in the argument, has been doing. (Fish 1972, 13)

Because the hermeneutic code of the self-help book involves a move from a question to an answer, it is "irreversible". Once the code has been revealed, it cannot be unrevealed; the reader, if the code is to have full effect, must follow its logico-temporal order, which means completing the quest for self-help now being set out (cf. Barthes 1974, 29–30). Returning to the self-help book, and rereading, to "find" the answer, will reveal nothing new. At any rate

> Emotional control [. . .] cannot be gained in any magical or easy way. You cannot develop it by merely reading a book. The only sure method is by working at it regularly, persistently. (Peale 1952, 89)

> The possession of the mere materials of knowledge is something very different from wisdom and understanding, which are reached through a higher kind of discipline than that of reading – which is often but a mere passive reception of other men's thoughts; there being little or no active effort of mind in the transaction. (Smiles 1859, 217–218)

To resolve the code of the self-help book means to part ways with the process of reading. What has been achieved – continuing with the metaphor – in reaching the last rung of the ladder has not been the accomplishment of self-help, but rather the knowledge that reading merely suspends that accomplishment. The tension arising from reading – that is, the lack of opportunity it affords the reader in the practical business of *doing* self-help – even when compensated by extratextual work, nevertheless falls short. Reading thus needs to be abandoned as a legitimate quest, being parasitic (on self-help book authors) in as much as it is a "mere passive reception of other men's thoughts". What is necessary for the reader to successfully produce as against receive self-help is that which the self-help book cannot supply: that is, the active role undertaken by interacting with the world, "working at it regularly, persistently". And so the reader is forced to return to the world beyond the self-help book to pursue a "higher kind of discipline"; the esoteric character of self-help constructed in the self-help book is reconfigured as the mundane practice of everyday life.

Conclusion

The normative characterisation of the self-help book as a "self-sufficient" textual form is present across a body of professional practice and research literature. This has been adopted unproblematically from the self-help book itself, and used as a resource for its practice and critique. It has sought to understand the self-help book in terms of an agency that claims ontological priority over those functions through which it assumes meaning – namely, reading. Thus, the self-help book continues to be treated as the agent of self-help.

In contrast I have drawn attention to this characterisation of the self-help book as part of a situated, rhetorical strategy that is deployed principally to attract a readership. Through a careful analytic reading, focusing on commonplace textual practices present across a corpus of texts, I have identified a tension around this self-characterised representation of the self-help book. First, I have underscored how the self-help book rhetorically attains a readership by convincing its readers that the temporally fixed and highly constrained period of reading is the requirement and condition for self-help. In following this process, spotlighting those conventions that guide its practice, I then situated this tension around the practice of reading, showing how readers are asked to supplement reading with extratextual work, specifically non-reading activities. Then, on completion of reading, readers experience the disappearance of the self-help book, as it points them away from the prioritisation of reading, to the temporally and pedagogically unspecified context of life beyond the self-help book.

What has been neglected by academic and professional treatments of the self-help book is any discussion of the paradox surrounding its own existence, which is to say the internally incoherent character of the textual form under discussion. Thus, the self-help book, by its own admission, has suggested its own insufficiency as a domain of practice of self-help, to the extent that it has deferred the reader, through reading, from his/her ongoing practical accomplishment of self-help in the context of everyday life.

Notes

1. UK-based outlets Amazon.co.uk, Publishers Weekly.com, and Waterstones.com all feature multiple self-help books on their bestsellers lists (all sources accessed 4 August 2007). A search on Amazon.co.uk for "self-help books", for instance, retrieves 42,106 hits.
2. Taken from Peale (1952).
3. Taken from Carlson (1997).
4. Taken from Lindenfield (2000, 70).
5. Taken from Lindenfield (2000, 70).

References

Adorno, T. 1994. *The stars down to earth: And other essays on the irrational culture.* London: Routledge.

Barthes, R. 1974. *S/Z.* Oxford: Blackwell Publishing.

Blackman, L. 2004. Self-help, media cultures and the production of female psychopathology. *European Journal of Cultural Studies* 7, no. 2: 219–36.

Carlson, R. 1997. *Don't sweat the small stuff ... and it's all small stuff.* London: Hodder & Stoughton.

Carnegie, D. 1936. *How to win friends and influence people.* New York: Pocket Books.

Dolby, S.K. 2005. *Self-help books: Why Americans keep reading them.* Chicago: University of Illinois Press.

Eco, U. 1979. *The role of the reader: Explorations in the semiotics of texts.* Bloomington: Indiana University Press.

———. 1992. Overinterpreting texts. In *Interpretation and overinterpretation,* ed. S. Collini, 45–67. Cambridge: Cambridge University Press.

Farrand, P. 2005. Development of a supported self help book prescription scheme in primary care. *Primary Care Mental Health* 3: 61–6.

Fish, S. 1972. *Self-consuming artfacts: The experience of seventeenth-century literature.* Berkeley: University of California.

Frude, N.J. 2004. A book prescription scheme in primary care. *Clinical Psychology* 39: 11–4.

Garfinkel, H. 1967. *Studies in ethnomethodology.* Englewood Cliffs, NJ: Prentice-Hall.

Genette, G. 1997. *Paratexts: Thresholds of interpretation.* Cambridge: Cambridge University Press.

Glasgow, R.E., and G.M. Rosen. 1978. Self-help behaviour therapy manuals: A review of self-help behaviour therapy manuals. *Psychological Bulletin* 85: 1–23.

Hansen, S., A. McHoul, and M. Rapley. 2003. *Beyond help: A consumers' guide to psychology.* Ross-on-Wye: PCCS Books.

Hazledon, R. 2003. Love yourself: The relationship of the self with itself in popular self-help texts. *Journal of Sociology* 39, no. 4: 413–28.

Holgate, S. 2005. Americans read millions of self-help books annually. http://usinfo.state.gov/xarchives/display.html?p=washfile-english&y=2005&m=June&x=20050606180405cpataruK0.3774378 (accessed 23 June 2007).

Justman, S. 2005. *Fool's paradise: The unreal world of pop psychology.* Chicago: Ivan R. Dee.

Lindenfield, G. 2000. *Self-esteem: Simple steps to develop self-worth and heal emotional wounds.* Berwick upon Tweed: Thorsons.

McGee, M. 2005. *Self-help, Inc. Makeover culture in American life.* Oxford: Oxford University Press.

McGraw, P. 1999. *Life strategies.* London: Vermilion.

McHoul, A. 1982. *Telling how texts talk: Essays on reading and ethnomethodology.* London: Routledge.

Peale, N.V. 1952. *The power of positive thinking.* New York: Fawcett Crest.

Peck, S.M. 2006 [1978]. *The road less travelled.* London: Arrow Books.

Pomerantz, A. 1986. Extreme case formulations: A new of legitimising claims. *Human Studies* 9: 219–30.

Rimke, H.M. 2000. Governing citizens through self-help literature. *Cultural Studies* 14, no. 1: 61–78.

Rose, N. 1990. *Governing the soul: The shaping of the private self.* London: Routledge.

Ruben, R. 1979. Uses of bibliotherapy in response to the 1970s. *Library Trends* 28, no. 2: 239–52.

Sacks, H. 1992. *Lectures on conversation.* Vols. 1 and 2., ed. G. Jefferson. Oxford: Blackwell.

Salerno, S. 2005. *SHAM: Self-help and actualization movement.* London: Nicholas Brealey Publishing.

Silove, D., and V. Manicavasagar. 1997. *Overcoming panic: A self-help guide using cognitive behavioural techniques.* London: Robinson.

Smiles, S. 1859. *Self-help: With illustrations of character and perseverance.* London: Institute of Economic Affairs.

Starker, S. 1986. Promises and prescriptions: Self-help book in mental health and medicine. *American Journal of Health Promotion* 1, no. 2: 19–25.

———. 1988. *Oracle at the supermarket: The American preoccupation with self-help books.* New Brunswick: Transaction.

———. 1990. Self-help books: Ubiquitous agents of health care. *Medical Psychotherapy* 3: 187–94.

Suchman, L. 2007. *Human–machine reconfigurations: Plans and situated actions*, 2nd edition. Cambridge: Cambridge University Press.

Tiede, T. 2001. *Self-help nation.* New York: Atlantic Monthly Press.

Woodstock, L. 2007. Think about it: The misbegotten promise of positive thinking discourse. *Journal of Communication Inquiry* 31, no. 2: 166–89.

"A very glamorized picture, that":[1] images of Scottish female herring workers on romance novel covers

Jane Liffen

This article analyses portrayals of Scottish female herring workers on the covers of romance novels and investigates how far these representations conform to, or subvert, the genre of romantic fiction. Covers are analysed to establish whether they accurately portray Scottish female herring workers at their labour. If romanticisation of the women's working role is evident, the ways in which this manifests itself and the possible reasons for this romanticisation are examined. Composition of images and the *mise-en-scène* of covers are analysed, as well as aspects concerning the narratives of the novels, and elements of herring processing work that are noticeably absent in the depictions are also considered. These elements excluded from the covers are examined through theory relating to the abject in an attempt to ascertain whether the covers potentially provide models of female empowerment for the reader.

Introduction

Scottish women travelled to ports on the east coast of England as itinerant workers gutting and packing herring in the open air from the late nineteenth century to the 1960s. Representations of these women workers have featured in contemporary historical romance novels, and images of female herring workers are used in the cultural packaging of these novels. Considering the messy nature of herring processing work, it seems unusual that romance novels have employed figures of Scottish female herring workers as main protagonists. This article explores the difficulties of appropriating these women workers as main characters through analysing covers of romance novels featuring images of Scottish female herring workers, and examining how far these representations conform to the genre of romance fiction.

Two romance novels featuring Scottish female herring workers will be analysed: *The Fisher Lass*[2] (Dickinson 2001) and *The Shimmer of the Herring* (Hood 2001). Both novel covers feature illustrations of women workers, and these are analysed to see whether they accurately portray Scottish female herring workers at their labour or whether romanticisation of the women's working role occurs. Figures on the covers are compared with main characters within the novels to determine whether the images truthfully reflect the narratives of the novels, and excerpts from oral history interviews with Scottish female herring workers supplement the textual readings.

Literature review

Romance fiction research has consisted of analytical positions that designate romance reading as either "'empowering' or [...] 'seductive'" (Moffitt 1993, 238). Radway had attempted to read the consumption of romances as a positive practice but states retrospectively that she had "unwittingly repeated the sexist assumption that has warranted a large portion of the commentary on romance. It was still motivated, that is, by the assumption that someone ought to worry responsibly about the effect of fantasy on women readers" (cited in Storey 1997, 152–153). Potential connections between the "idealized association of men with chivalry and heroism" and the limitation of "women's personal power aspirations", labelled the "glass slipper effect", suggest that romance reading may work to reinforce gender stereotypes (Rudman and Heppen 2003, 1359). This is demonstrated in "nurse-novels", consisting of love affairs between nurses and doctors, and romance novels from the mid-1960s onwards that positioned heroines in predominantly "'female' occupations (secretary, teacher, governess)" (Markert 1985, 72).

Conversely, as cited by O'Connor and Klaus (2000, 376), "Ang (1988) [...] held that fantasy [...] can be a site of resistance to patriarchal demands since it entails a playful and enjoyable way of transcending reality". Modleski (1982) also suggests romance fiction is potentially subversive in its use of revenge narratives in which the heroine eventually exerts power over the hero and he submits to her will. In a study of Christian and secular romance fiction in the United States, heroes of secular novels are identified as financially powerful and physically strong characters who then become "tamed" by the emotional strength of female protagonists (Clawson 2006). The examination of this interplay of power between hero and heroine has been a central feature of romance fiction research. As stated by Gill and Herdieckerhoff (2006, 490): "Assiter (1988) suggests that [...] both heterosexual pornography and romantic fiction eroticise the power relations between the sexes". Brackett (2000) also analyses power interactions between men and women relating to the ways in which romance fiction readers deal with external criticisms concerning the reading of romance novels.

Owen states that publishers and authors consider there to be two main types of romance fiction novels that may be distinguished by their covers: "'strong' romances featuring a picture of a woman in the foreground with a small figure of a man often somewhere behind her left shoulder, soft romances portraying a couple usually embracing" (1997, 537). A romance scenario describing "the girl of humble birth who eventually marries the all-powerful Prince" is a part of a soft romance narrative, displaying "what overtly seems like the most stereotyped picture of patriarchal, heterosexual relationships", whilst the "strong" romance "foregrounds a strong, self-confident, resourceful woman" (Owen 1997, 537–538). The novel covers featuring images of Scottish female herring workers follow "strong" romance cover conventions, reflecting the strength of character of the main female protagonists.

The present article will firstly analyse the covers of both novels in terms of composition of the images, including the positioning of figures and potential significance of compositional choices. Secondly, the *mise-en-scène* of the images and text incorporated in the cover packaging is examined in order to ascertain the significance of what is included. Finally, absences relating to the work of the women and reasons for the omission of certain aspects of herring processing labour within cover images will be explored psychoanalytically in an effort to understand the cultural choices made by publishers in the marketing of these novels.

Cover composition

The cover image of *The Fisher Lass* depicts a herring gutting yard scene in which a female figure is foregrounded and behind her left shoulder a male figure is positioned in the background, conforming to the "strong" romance novel cover formula (Owen 1997, 537).

Both characters rest their hands on the barrels in front of them; their adoption of similar postures connotes their potential connection with one another. The body of the foregrounded female figure is turned slightly to her left and, although her smile is not actually directed at the male figure, this enables it to be observed by him. The female herring worker adopts a half-profile facial position that is frequently employed in the depiction of heroines on the covers of romance novels. Drawing on Victoroff's categorisation of illustrations, Paizis suggests that the half-profile characterises an individual connected to the realms of feeling, rather than one directly petitioning for the reader's empathy as a face-on figure might. The ambiguity of the pose encourages the reader to "participate in the private/shared adventure" of the main protagonist's journey, drawing out the reader's own emotional desires and aspirations (Paizis 1998, 53).

Signifying her psychic separation from her surroundings, the central female figure is positioned slightly away from her co-workers and the male figure beyond. Her eyes, averted to a point beyond the boundary of the image, suggest that her thoughts lie elsewhere. The imaginary is privileged over reality in this instance and will be mirrored within the narrative of the novel as the aspirations of the main protagonist, Jeannie, will triumph over the harsh, practical surroundings of the gutting yard.

In *The Fisher Lass* there is an element of the "Cinderella" narrative with regard to Jeannie's journey, as she eventually leaves behind her fisher beginnings and marries a middle-class merchant. Although the cover conforms to "strong" romance compositional conventions, aspects of "soft" romance are also inherent within the text, reflecting her shifting status and problematising the novel's categorisation. Jeannie's aspiration to leave her work behind is reflected in the cover image, as the figure looks not at the man in the background, whose clothing denotes a manual labourer, but beyond the frame of the picture. This mirrors the main character's dreams which lie away from her immediate vicinity and the work "of those born to the fishing way of life", as the back cover of the novel states.

In an alternative reading, the presence of the male figure on the cover invites the reader to look at the main female protagonist from a masculine perspective. This joining of the gazes of male figure and reader creates a united admiration for the main protagonist and reinforces her quality of "to-be-looked-at-ness". It could be argued that the gaze of the male figure also acts to confirm the reader's own ability to attract attention from members of the dominant order. Through his "looking after" her, he becomes a symbolic nurturer and the female figure's struggle within the narrative is consequently imbued with worth through a representative of patriarchal power validating her position. This may be in opposition to the reality of the reader positioned in a society in which masculine expressions of nurturing are not encouraged: "[...] by emphasizing the intensity of the hero's uninterrupted gaze [...] the fantasy [...] evokes the memory of a period in the reader's life when she was the centre of a profoundly nurturant individual's attention" (Radway 1994, 84).

Owen (1997, 541) states that in romances "although the heroine's looks are minutely described they are vague in character. It is as though the heroine is a template on to which the reader can project her own self". The man's gaze is directed at the main female figure, representative of his concern with the factual life of his surroundings within the confines of the image, whilst she smiles at an unknown person or situation off-cover. The female's gaze directed elsewhere is indexical of her identification with the unseen, and, by extension, reflective of the reader's empathy with matters beyond physical reality.

In contrast, on the cover of *The Shimmer of the Herring*, the central figure of a female herring worker is positioned alone in the foreground, signifying the main character's isolation. The sea can be seen over her left shoulder, where Owen suggests a small figure of a man should be present in order to fulfil the criteria of a "strong" romance novel cover. Instead of a male figure, a sailed drifter boat occupies the space. In the narrative of the novel, Bethany, a shore worker, longs to go to sea, a desire that subverts the gender rules of the fishing community in which she lives; even though she owns part of a drifter inherited from her father, she is not allowed to work at the fishing on the boat. In this instance, the boat replaces the male love interest in the cover image. This identification of the boat as the object of Bethany's desire may propose a potential yearning for maternal nurturance, as opposed to the fantasy of masculine nurturing, which is usually offered in romance fiction: "gendered ideas pervaded the fishery. The sea itself was female, as is common throughout the North Atlantic. So were the fishing boats" (Nadel-Klein 2003, 54). This is supported by the theory that the appeal of romance fiction:

> lies in seeing the hero as a "male mother". Many critics base their analyses on Chodorow's (1978) work, which suggests that daughters make an incomplete separation from their mothers and therefore spend their lives yearning for nurturing. (Owen 1997, 541)

If this is the case, it follows that identification occurs between reader and cover image, and, by extension, the main character of the novel, as well as wanting to subvert gender-defined labour categories, reflects the reader's desire for fulfilment of self-nurture. Nadel-Klein's identification of fishing boats as feminine suggests that the yearning for sailing on Bethany's part could be identified as a wish to be surrounded once more in a womb of motherly love. This desire for plenitude may mirror that of the reader in her identification with the main protagonist, and reading romances offer a temporary fulfilment of this desire, which in reality, in terms of romantic love, is arguably denied by a patriarchal allegiance to rigid gender-defined roles:

> Chodorow maintains [...] male children [...] tend to separate more completely from their mothers by suppressing their own emotionality and capacities for tenderness which they associate with mothers and femininity. The resulting asymmetry in human personality, she concludes, leads to a situation where men typically cannot fulfil all of a woman's emotional needs. (Radway 1983, 61)

Romance novels potentially compensate for this perceived male inability to nurture by imbuing male romantic lead characters with a capacity to empathise with the female protagonist whilst maintaining an ultra-masculine persona (Radway 1983). The male mother possesses a capacity for positive action and for nurture, qualities potentially inherent within the main protagonist herself and, by extension, the reader, yet projected outwards onto a male figure. Whilst Treacher (1988) holds that firm gender identities are key to the success of romantic fiction, the idea of the "male mother" problematises this viewpoint. It is the roles of female characters within romance fiction that are perhaps more rigidly gendered.

Mise-en-scène and romanticised images

Many romance novel cover illustrations share the characteristic of a photo-realistic style that mimics figurative, lifelike scenes whilst retaining a quality of painterliness. This varies between novels, with the cover of *The Shimmer of the Herring* displaying a greater closeness to reality than the more painterly image of *The Fisher Lass*, in which only the face of the main female character possesses a photo-realistic quality. This illustrative style is metonymic of a dreamlike state in which the fantasy world of romance fiction connects with real life, and is specifically employed in romance fiction covers. It is argued that a purely photographic cover would not enable the same transition from reality to fantasy for the reader of the novel (Paizis 1998). This is in contrast with the photographic images of erotic novels, such as the Black Lace texts which feature more explicit sexual description within the stories. The photographic images suggest the novels reflect a narrative detailing the physicality of the relationships. Erotic novel covers that display "a solitary woman posed as an object to be looked at" in a photographic cover-image style, perhaps unwittingly reflect a greater reality in terms of a continued "imbalance in sexual power relations, which, even in fantasy militate against an active female gaze" (Sonnet 1999, 181). The romance novel's illustration potentially allows for a more effective transition to fantasy than the erotic novel cover, even though this fantasy realm is also negotiated through patriarchal notions of femininity. The fantasy world of the romance novel and reality is then mediated through the cover image. In a study of adolescent readers of romance, "the reading practice involves [. . .] a pseudoexperience of the real [. . .] reality becomes the image, making the readers no longer actors but actually a part of the text" (Moffitt 1993, 246).

In Radway's *Reading the Romance*, a reader of romantic fiction "patiently explained, a good cover is dependent on the artist's 'having read the book and at least if you're going to draw the characters, have the right hair colour'" (1994, 109). This continuity is important to readers because a cover corroborating with the story inside it lends authority to the fantasy world of the narrative "by giving concrete form to that world *designated* by the book's language" (Radway 1994, 109). The female herring worker on the cover of *The Fisher Lass* has striking red hair, faithfully depicting the hair colour of the main character of the novel, and thus setting up a correlation between the cover and the narrative itself. The romance novel cover of *The Fisher Lass* contains back-cover information emphasising struggle inherent within the narrative. This is in opposition to the cover image, which portrays a scene devoid of conflict in which the main female figure wears a smile. The additional cover information is markedly dramatic, describing "a love story as powerful and restless as the mighty North Sea", promoting an incongruity between words and image that problematises meaning. It is claimed this disharmony provokes anxiety within its reader, which may be assuaged by reading the novel (Paizis 1998). Yet, beyond this initial mismatch there is more incongruence inherent within the cover relating to the disparity between the depiction of a "concrete form" of the world of the novel and the Scottish female herring worker's reality: the illustrations are actually fantasies of female herring workers' labour. It is ironic that the women's work takes the guise of a metaphorical "reality" on the covers over and above the physicality of the everyday experience of herring processing.

When I showed the cover of *The Fisher Lass* to a former Scottish female herring worker, she remarked that the main figure's scarf "would have been hanging in the barrel ... if she bent over". This comment suggests the cover images are, to some extent, romanticised with regard to the depiction of their clothing. The same woman stated that the scarf draped over the flowing hair of the figure illustrated on the cover of *The Shimmer of the Herring* looked "too glamorous [...] you didn't have all that hair [...] that would have been all over our eyes before you know where you were" (interview with "Annie", 2004). Although scarves of the kind worn by the cover figure were also worn by Scottish female herring workers, particularly in the late nineteenth and early twentieth centuries, the soft drape with which they are styled in the cover images bears little relation to the tight snug fit demanded by the practicalities of the women's working lives. The looseness and flow of the garments in the images are metonymic of the changeable feminine flow ascribed to the women embarking on a journey of self-discovery in the narratives. The female figure in the cover image of *The Shimmer of the Herring* is situated on the seashore, alongside flowing water also indexical of the liminal position of the female itinerant herring worker. This positioning of the figure, coupled with a lack of industrial motifs, connects the herring worker within the image to the natural world. In reality, organisation of labour was governed by a desire for maximum profitability from the workforce, and within gutting yards situated away from the shore, troughs, known as "farlins", were positioned in rows and work was governed by piecework rates. Through the illustration denying the industrial aspect of herring processing, which the novel itself includes, the cover conveys an alignment of the female figure with the natural world that strengthens patriarchal-ascribed notions of femininity:

> The feminine character, and the ideal of femininity on which it is modelled, are products of masculine society. The image of undistorted nature arises only in distortion, as its opposite. Where it claims to be humane, masculine society breeds in woman its own corrective, and shows itself through this limitation implacably the master. The feminine character is a negative imprint of domination. But therefore equally bad. Whatever is in the context of bourgeois delusion called nature, is merely the scar of social mutilation. (Adorno, cited in Warner 1985, 325)

The cover of *The Shimmer of the Herring* predominantly uses similar muted colours to *The Fisher Lass* cover. A bright pink is used for the author's name and subheading lettering, corresponding to similar tones in the red lips of the female figure and the heads of the dead herrings she holds in front of her in a basket. There is also reddening on the fingers of her right hand as she grips the basket. The colour of the heads of the fish is produced when blood is released from their bodies. By this colour corresponding to the female figure's lips, a connection between death and passion is made. The red lips of the main protagonist show they are blood-filled and connotative of passion, yet that passion corresponds with the dead fish she carries through their shared colour, suggesting her desire will not be sustained or allowed to flourish. This is supported by the connection, through colour identification, with the words of the subheading: "The call of the sea. The pull of the heart." The correspondence of the colour of the dead fish and the lettering demonstrates that the figure's desire to go to sea is not allowed to flourish and the "pull" remains a "call" unanswered. The language employed by the subheading in its referencing of "the heart" is romantic, and reinforces the previously argued notion that the boat represents a substitute for a romantic relationship.

On seeing the cover of *The Shimmer of the Herring*, the same former Scottish herring worker said the cover figure "looks like someone that has been dressed up" (interview with "Annie", 2004). Her terminology suggests that the cover figure is more akin to an actress who might be playing the part of a herring worker rather than an image of a woman familiar with fish processing work. In their identification with the figure on the cover, who is playing at being a herring worker, the romance readership are embracing the role of Scottish female herring worker, but in a guise that does not fully assume the reality of the work, and at times is at odds with the narrative of the novel. There are aspects of the women's work that are conspicuously omitted from the images, and their absence is potentially just as significant as that which has been included within the novel covers.

Herring processing work was carried out in crews of three, with two women gutting herring and one packing fish into barrels. The main protagonists of both romance novels are gutters, however the cover images show packers as the central female figures. According to a former Scottish female herring worker who worked packing barrels, gutters often helped the packer in their crew if they were ahead in their gutting work and so it is possible a gutter could temporarily pack herring too (interview with "Mary", 2005). Yet the cover figure of *The Fisher Lass* is working as a packer whilst female figures gut fish in the background, precluding her from a gutting role within the crew. The image of *The Shimmer of the Herring* is without any depiction of herring innards, yet mess would be incurred in the role of a gutter. Apart from almost imperceptible traces of reddish brown on the forearms and pinafore of the central figure of *The Fisher Lass*, there is no evidence of herring gutting work with regard to the foregrounded characters. The lack of detritus within the *mise-en-scène* of both novel covers, and the absence of knives used for gutting, are important in the construction of the images' meanings.

Omission of knives

The dead fish within both images, whilst denoting the physical realm of the gutting yard, simultaneously signify the end of life and separation from the realm of physicality. By including a knife in the image, the transition from reality into the imaginary world of romance fiction may be undermined; as an object that cuts flesh, a gutting knife would potentially draw the reader back to the tangible world she inhabits, both through its signification of reality from which romance readers seek to escape, and also through its role as signifier of labour. In this sense, the depiction of gutting on the novel cover might problematise romance reading's attempt to provide a nurturing fantasy relationship for the reader.

In the narrative the main protagonist of *The Fisher Lass* wields her gutting knife in the face of a man who will eventually become her husband. Her action is fuelled by "passionate hatred" and "violence" of feelings that shock her (Dickinson 2001, 62). In her physical expression of anger, the main protagonist takes on a masculine role that problematises romance novel principles – but because her anger is in response to an incident of male aggression that occurs earlier on in the narrative, she continues to conform to an accepted role within romance novels of mistreated heroine:

> [R]eaders [...] instead of admitting reservations about the overtly aggressive nature of a heroine's behaviour [...] focused instead on the unjustified nature of the hero's actions. [...] Given the vehemence of their reaction, it seems possible that the male violence that does occur in romances may actually serve as an opportunity to express anger which is otherwise repressed and ignored. (Radway 1983, 70)

The fact that the female protagonist of *The Fisher Lass* is expressing her anger in a physically aggressive way contrasts with the constructed femininity of the figure on the novel cover. There are other moments within the narratives that exemplify force, such as the successful organisation of strike action among women herring workers in *The Shimmer of the Herring*. Similarly, this subversive element of the novel is at odds with the simplified portrayal on the cover.

An example of acceptance of a constructed feminine position occurs when the heroine of *The Fisher Lass* gives up her gutting job. The gutting yard is initially a site of resistance in which she earns economic independence, which is then abandoned for an acceptance of Robert's domain in the form of his house, and the accompanying domesticity. The knife in this instance is representative of a relative autonomy. Yet, as a symbol of action in a cover image, even in a "strong" romance, a knife would excessively problematise gendered spheres of behaviour that prescribe female as passive and male as active.

The presence of a knife would also signify domination over the natural world, of which the herring are indexical, and therefore subvert the idea that the women of the covers are aligned with nature and at the mercy of a masculine-defined idea of femininity. The knife in these instances might also represent weaponry, reclaimed from an order which Adorno states, as previously quoted, is responsible for the "scars of social mutilation" associated with the patriarchal construct of the feminine character.

Edinger pronounces that the archetypal figure of the spiritual father relates to "images of piercing and penetration" signified by, among other symbols, a knife (Edinger, cited in Ulanov 1978, 61). In this analogy, the presence of a blade would give female figures access to a masculine power that would threaten gender boundaries. As opposed to the wielding of the knife in anger, in the action of gutting this power is used transformatively to enable life-giving sustenance to be reclaimed from the bodies of dead herring, preserving them for food. In this way the masculine and the feminine come together, pointing to a collaboration of power.

Omission of detritus

The idealised portrayals of female herring workers in the cover images are devoid of the mess that accompanies their labour, elevating them above the physical realm and paradoxically positioning them in opposition to the body, even though they are located in close proximity to herring bodies. In denying the depiction of detritus, the image "veils the squalor of sensual reality" and, in doing so, "an idealised version of the woman as beauty is wielded against a debased image of her as sensuality" (Eagleton 1990, 117). Whilst the presence of red lips and flowing scarves are signs of sensual experience that are permitted within the cover images, blood and detritus would confuse the genre through their anomalous status and threaten not only the constructed femininity of the figures of the novels but also the prescribed boundaries of romance novels:

> The abject (including tears, saliva, faeces, urine, vomit, mucus) marks bodily sites which will later become erotogenic zones (mouth, eyes, anus, nose, genitals). The subject must expel these abjects to establish the "clean and proper" body of oedipalization. Yet they cannot be expelled, for they remain the preconditions of corporeal, material existence. (Grosz 1992, 198)

The lack of guts on the kwytes (protective aprons) of the women workers of the covers may represent a pre-menstruating female, devoid of the potentiality to take on "an inescapable 'abject' status that accompanies the maternal" (Kristeva 1995, 120). Similarly, if open bodies of herring and evidence of fish innards were depicted on the aprons and kwytes of figures on the cover images, connections between the female figures and menstruation and sexual maturity might be signified. However, any abject material is conspicuously absent.

A transgression of limits and symbolic bodily extension occurs through the displacement of innards onto the clothes of the female herring worker whilst she works. In this instance, the liminality of herring blood is emphasised in relation to its new position; what was once a life force inside the herring shifts onto the protective clothing and becomes dirt because of its new location: "dirt is essentially disorder. There is no such thing as absolute dirt: it exists in the eye of the beholder [...] Dirt offends against order" (Douglas 1966, 2). If the cover images contain dirt, a transgression of boundaries and order takes place. Depicted on the kwytes of the women workers of the covers, the guts would constitute "matter out of place", due to the fact that they are no longer contained inside the herring (Douglas 1966, 40). In this way not only would the transgression of bodily boundaries occur, but also the idea of woman as essence of cleanliness would be undermined. The women workers of the image would no longer embody the constructed feminine attribute of physical purity (Cresswell 1996).

The abject quality of detritus on the clothes of Scottish female herring workers mirrors the taboo surrounding menstrual blood that also relates to ideas of pollution. In contemporary Western society, this concept is demonstrated through advertising campaigns highlighting the discreetness of a company's featured sanitary protection and advertisements past and present are "full of dire warnings about odour" (Houppert 2000, 34). As odour is considered transgressive in constructed notions of femininity, so description of fish smells is excluded in romance fiction, partly due to smell being deemed "a pervasive and invisible presence difficult to regulate" (Stallybrass and White 1986, 139). It is only when the main protagonist of *The Fisher Lass* decides to be with the man she loves that the novel refers to "the aroma of fish that she had lived with for the whole of her life", at the point she abandons it by throwing away her old clothes (Dickinson 2001, 341). As the smell of fish is considered essentially transgressive, it is not until she gives up her work that a public declaration of love between the central character and someone beyond the confines of the fishing community can take place.

Later in the narrative of *The Fisher Lass,* Jeannie complies with gender conventions, voluntarily conforming to the dominant middle-class order to which her future husband belongs, as she embraces new underwear, styled hair and expensive clothes: "just for today she felt as if she had stepped off the front cover of a fashion magazine" (Dickinson 2001, 341). In letting go of her "fisher-girlness", she adopts a position in which spectacle, deemed masculine, is valued over other senses, such as smell (Cresswell 1996). Just as the main protagonist changes, so the cover is sanitised of the detritus that accompanies herring processing work, providing a socially acceptable image of the heroine for the reader.

Images of women workers gutting herring in the open air would establish connections with menstruation through the shared abject status of fish innards and menstrual blood. There are also similarities in their constitution: herring detritus consists not only of guts but blood and scales, whilst menstrual blood is made up of "some blood, but it also contains the broken-down uterine lining, mucus from the vagina and other fluids" (Walker 1997, 11). Gutting is referred to as "cleaning" the fish, in contrast with the symbolic quality associated with menstruation's capacity as polluting agency. The act of gutting demonstrates an uncanny birth in which fish innards are born into the world from the dead body of a herring.

Conclusion

If foregrounded female herring gutters were present in the cover images, with all the abject elements of their labour, they might allude to an autonomy associated with ideas of a mythic matriarchal power, in which signifiers of "woman-dominated society" include "darkness, wetness and the changing moon (as opposed to the sun) and [are] intimately linked with both reproductive and sexual aspects of female physiology" (Knight 1991, 421–422). Not only are all these elements associated with herring fishing – in that the fish are caught at night at sea and the "herring moon" at the autumn fishing season in East Anglia represented an auspicious time for landing catches (Ommanney 1965, 123–124) – but also gutting work potentially shares common characteristics with menstruation with regard to hidden realms, both in physical and cultural terms, being brought out into the world.

Although the narratives themselves contain subversive elements, the portrayal of these through cover images is forbidden. An open female body, the grotesque body, is "abjected from the bodily canons of classical aesthetics. [. . .] open, protruding, irregular, secreting, multiple and changing; it is identified with non-official 'low' culture or the carnivalesque, and with social transformation" (Russo 1994, 8). The abject maternal body on the cover of a romance novel would potentially act as an agent for social change. Just as the dead bodies of fish are transformed into life-giving food, so a depiction of gutting herring on the cover of a romance novel might also reflect a birth of a new social order, enabling the exclusive realms of romance relationships and constructed gender positions of women in romance novels to open to the flow of negotiation.

The nature of herring processing work problematises notions of an allegiance to a constructed feminine position that is integral to the formulation of cover images of romance novels. The presence of innards and knives on the covers would conceivably portray a transgression of boundaries that mirrors "Kristeva's refusal to use biological categories in deciding who is what kind of gendered subject" (Cameron 1992, 174). This would not only subvert romance fiction conventions but may also facilitate an opportunity for readers, paradoxically, to transcend the language of the symbolic order. A feminine subject position, in the Kristevan sense inhabited by one whose "repression of pre-Oedipal elements is less than complete", potentially offers a greater propensity to access that which lies beyond "rational discourse" (Cameron 1992, 174).

In romance fiction's privileging of emotional desire and imaginary worlds over intellectual and physical concerns, it "validates feelings rather than logic" in its position as "the one genre written primarily by women, for women" (Tunon 1995, 473). Yet, by excluding gutting knives and detritus from covers, female figures within the images retain a constructed feminine position, whilst the presence of a "male mother" (or a "male mother" substitute) compensates for the lack of the maternal. The covers exemplify how positive aspects of constructed masculine behaviour, as well as the maternal, are generally disallowed to female figures, even though this is at times disputed in some of the novels themselves. It is perhaps through a female protagonist negotiating with these aspects and breaking the boundaries of a constructed femininity ascribed to them in romance novels and on their covers that a greater embrace of loving kindness may be possible that extends beyond all boundaries.

The present article has supplemented a textual analysis with some references to oral histories and, in doing so, further illuminates the conditions of gender relations with reference to romance fiction covers through the authority of Scottish female herring workers' voices. These comments not only offer insights into the particular form of femininity prescribed by the covers, but also go beyond the realms of fiction, conveying gender relations pertaining to the lived experience of women who worked in the herring industry.

Notes

1. Former Scottish female herring worker's response when shown the cover image of *The Shimmer of the Herring*, written by Evelyn Hood (interview with "Annie", 2004).
2. Women workers were known as "fisher lasses" or "fisher girls", regardless of their age, and women workers also used these terms to describe themselves.

References

Ang, I. 1988. Feminist desire and female pleasure: On Janice Radway's *Reading the romance: woman, patriarchy and popular literature*. In Television and the Female Consumer, ed. D. Mann and L. Spigel. *Camera Obscura* special issue 16: 179–90.

Assiter, A. 1988. Romance fiction: Porn for women? In *Perspectives on pornography: Sexuality in film and literature*, ed. G. Day and C. Bloom, 101–9. Basingstoke Macmillan.

Brackett, K. 2000. Facework strategies among romance fiction readers. *The Social Science Journal* 37: 347–60.

Cameron, D. 1992. *Feminism and linguistic theory*. Basingstoke: Macmillan.

Chodorow, N. 1978. *The reproduction of mothering*. Berkeley: University of California Press.

Clawson, L. 2006. Cowboys and schoolteachers: Gender in romance novels, secular and Christian. *Sociological Perspectives* 48: 461–79.

Cresswell, T. 1996. *In place/out of place*. Minneapolis: University of Minnesota.

Dickinson, M. 2001. *The fisher lass*. London: Macmillan.

Douglas, M. 1966. *Purity and danger*. London: Routledge and Kegan Paul.

Eagleton, T. 1990. *The ideology of the aesthetic*. Oxford: Blackwell.

Gill, R., and E. Herdieckerhoff. 2006. Rewriting the romance. *Feminist Media Studies* 6: 487–504.

Grosz, E. 1992. Julia Kristeva. In *Feminism and psychoanalysis: A critical dictionary*, ed. E. Wright, 194–200. Oxford: Blackwell.

Hood, E. 2001. *The shimmer of the herring*. London: Warner Books.

Houppert, K. 2000. *The curse: Confronting the last unmentionable taboo: Menstruation*. London: Profile.

Knight, C. 1991. *Blood relations: Menstruation and the origins of culture*. London: Yale University Press.

Kristeva, J. 1995. *New maladies of the soul*. New York: Columbia University Press.

Markert, J. 1985. Romance publishing and the production of culture. *Poetics* 14: 69–93.

Modleski, T. 1982. *Loving with a vengeance: Mass-produced fantasies for women*. New York: Routledge.

Moffitt, M. 1993. Articulating meaning: Reconceptions of the meaning process, fantasy/reality, and identity in leisure activities. *Communication Theory* 3: 231–51.

Nadel-Klein, J. 2003. *Fishing for heritage*. Oxford: Berg.

O'Connor, B., and E. Klaus.. 2000. Pleasure and meaningful discourse: An overview of research issues. *International Journal of Cultural Studies* 3: 369–87.

Ommanney, F. 1965. *A draught of fishes*. London: Longmans Green.

Owen, M. 1997. Re-inventing romance: Reading popular romantic fiction. *Women's Studies International Forum* 20: 537–46.

Paizis, G. 1998. *Love and the novel: The poetics and politics of romantic fiction*. Basingstoke: Macmillan.

Radway, J. 1983. Women read the romance: The interaction of text and context. *Feminist Studies* 9: 53–78.

———. 1994. *Reading the romance: Women, patriarchy and popular literature.* London: Verso.

Rudman, L., and J. Heppen. 2003. Implicit romantic fantasies and women's interest in personal power: A glass slipper effect? *Personality and Social Psychology Bulletin* 29: 1357–70.

Russo, M. 1994. *The female grotesque.* New York: Routledge.

Sonnet, E. 1999. Erotic fiction by women for women: The pleasures of post-feminist heterosexuality. *Sexualities* 2: 167.

Stallybrass, P., and A. White. 1986. *The politics and poetics of transgression.* New York: Cornell University.

Storey, J. 1997. *An introduction to cultural theory and popular culture.* Hemel Hempstead: Prentice Hall.

Treacher, A. 1988. What is life without my love? Desire and romantic fiction. In *Sweet dreams: Sexuality, gender and popular fiction,* ed. S. Radstone, 73–90. London: Lawrence and Wishart.

Tunon, J. 1995. An appetite for romance: How to understand, buy, display and promote romance fiction. *Library Acquisitions: Practice and Theory* 19: 471–5.

Ulanov, A. 1978. *The feminine in Jungian psychology and in Christian theology.* Evanston, IL: Northwestern University Press.

Walker, A. 1997. *The menstrual cycle.* London: Routledge.

Warner, M. 1985. *Monuments and maidens.* London: Weidenfeld and Nicolson.

Sex in the sun: racial stereotypes and tabloid news

Michael Pickering

Sexuality and ethnicity are potent categories, especially in combination. In news reporting, the ways in which such categories are symbolically mobilised may seem very much of the present, but such uses are often deeply rooted in the past and reproduce stock notions that were developed in previous historical formations. The present article takes a front-page tabloid news story as an example of how this can operate. It shows how the story draws on various stereotypical representations of female and black sexuality on the one hand, white European and black African social arrangements on the other. Its narrative structure privileges and silences certain "voices" in the narrative, and uses what these "voices" say to support its key thematic template. The discourse of the story is schematically organised around this template, which deals in long-established binary conceptions of civilisation and primitiveness, and strategically opposed values of social responsibility and personal fulfilment. These are reinforced not only by the various textual features of the narrative, but also by its intertextual relation to the other, subsidiary, front-page story in the same edition of the newspaper. The lead story plays fear and fascination off against each other as its key point of interest, and in doing so ensures that various gender and racial myths and stereotypes are maintained in ideological circulation.

Introduction

Black men are pearls in beauteous ladies' eyes. (*Two Gentlemen of Verona*)

One of the paradoxes of the news is that it is not new at all. News reporting is always about some recent event, but the manner in which reporting occurs conforms to long-established values and practices. This is a widely acknowledged feature of news journalism. Numerous studies have shown how it deals in short-term changes through narrative codes, formats and genres that change only on a gradual basis. In forms of discourse that focus on the transient and fleeting developments that fly up from one day and one week to the next, certain enduring ways of depicting other people or cultures are readily facilitated by news conventionalism. In this way, the regularised production routines and the familiar structures of news discourse that account for the high degree of standardisation in news stories are conducive to the reproduction of various forms of stereotype, even when particular individuals are identified and named.

Stereotypes are closely suited to the ways news handles what is temporally proximate through stock narrative templates. They are similarly paradoxical because they appear to operate as essentialist markers and reductive fixities in direct relation to current events and issues, but are in most cases figures of representation with long tentacular roots into the past. They seem to "fit the moment" yet at the same time are actively residual elements of broad historical configurations of social encounter, order, domination and control. Their resilience and periodic reappearance are what are most remarkable, rather than their immediate manifestations in any specific instance of news construction and narration.[1]

We have, of course, to attend to this resilience, at least in part, through such immediate manifestations; and in doing so in this article I want to show how the durability of stereotypical figures and associations is given new support and impetus by being re-dressed and updated through the details supplied by a particular "of the moment" story.[2] The story was given front-page prominence in a tabloid newspaper of the last decade of the twentieth century (see Figure 1). It concerned adultery and the abandonment of her husband and family home by a middle-aged white woman, Sandra Anderson, who fell in love with a young black man, Sagnia Bakary, while on holiday in Sarrakunda, a Gambian seaside resort, having gone to him initially for horse-riding lessons. The *Sun*, Britain's leading tabloid at the time, made this its lead story for Monday 7 February 1994, giving it priority over all the other available stories for this particular edition.[3] These included the massacre of 68 people in Sarajevo, attacks on John Major's premiership as leader of the Tory party, even a nude hang-glider landing on the roof of Buckingham Palace. These were all written up in the inside pages but were not given the top treatment reserved for this story about inter-racial sex and a broken marriage. The story was elaborated over one and a half pages inside the newspaper (see later Figures 2 and 3).

Structure of the text

Aside from its front-page status, the importance attached to the story was emphasised by three textual features: first, the banner headline consisting of two-inch black capital letters, and contrasting with the other headlines on the front page, which were either in colour, white, lower-case or smaller font; second, the "*Sun* Exclusive" tag given to the story; and third, the use of a photograph illustration of the woman in the story, which again contrasts with the other story included on the front page. While the story was placed on the bottom

Figure 1.   Bottom half of the front page of the *Sun* for Monday 7 February 1994.

Figure 2. Page 5 of the *Sun* for Monday 7 February 1994, continuing the story begun on the front page, using colour photographs and an illustration.

half of the front page, it attained centrality because of the words "MUD-HUT RAT", which figure in the centre of the page, immediately attracting the eye and leading straight through to the succeeding words "STOLE MY WIFE". The banner headline was wrapped around the initial paragraph of the story, itself given emphasis by the bold font: "A HEARTBROKEN businessman told yesterday how his wife dumped him to live in a mud hut with a native she met on an African holiday". Following the conventional pyramidal structure of news narrative, this short paragraph contained the gist of the story, giving further meaning to the headline and the subsidiary headline at the bottom of the page: "Husband Ditched After Sunshine African Holiday". The compositional centrality of the paragraph in the story's layout, surrounded by the headline and image of the woman in question, reinforced its narrative centrality, its quality as the nucleus of the story. This condensed the general theme of the story into its most significant components, with the

At home in England...Sandra said life was "hell" before she quit

Sun EXCLUSIVE

From HILARY DOUGLAS in Gambia

RUNAWAY mum Sandra Anderson spoke for the first time of her exotic affair and said: "It's like a mix of Shirley Valentine and Out of Africa — with more romance."

Stirring a pot on an open fire outside the shack she now calls home, she added: "I'm so happy, I've never really been happy before but this is like paradise on earth."

Sandra, 39, moved into African prince Sagnia Bakary's spartan shack a month ago after leaving her family in Leominster, Hereford and Worcester.

It is set in the middle of the Gambian bush about 15 miles from the coastal resort of Sarrakunda. The hut has no running water and the loo is a hole in the ground outside.

But Sandra insisted: "It's better than a five star hotel.

"It's basic, there's an open cesspit in the garden but I'm happy." She went on:

● My husband Frank made my life hell. He's a very difficult man to live with, but here I feel like a princess.

Brilliant

Frank never bothered about me at all — he just took me for granted and kept telling me I was worthless.

Baks makes me feel like a real woman. I've lost a stone since I've been here — eating well, the sunshine and all the exercise I'm getting, if you know what I mean.

Baks is a brilliant lover. For the first time in my life I've got a man who actually bothers to get me turned on and worries about me in bed.

Frank never did any of this and sex wasn't something I enjoyed.

Now it's wonderful, I have this lovely double bed I had made locally — it's heaven.

The minute I saw Baks riding down the beach towards me on the first day of our holiday here in Gambia I fell for him right away. I didn't think there was any chance.

LOO IS A HOLE IN GROUND BUT I'VE FOUND PARADISE

He treated me so well, was so courteous and a real gentleman. I knew he was the man for me.

Dreamed

Now we're running a riding school together. And I've never been happier.

I've always dreamed of being whisked away in the sunshine by a man on a horse and now it's happened.

I just can't believe it and have to pinch myself every morning to show I'm not dreaming.

Sandra's only regret is being separated from sons Robert and Gavin.

She said: "I miss them every day and write to them all the time.

"I've told them they're welcome to come and see me out here, and I do intend going back to see them

some time in the future.

"They were very upset at first but now understand that I'm totally happy for the first time.

"When they do come out here I'm sure that within a few minutes they'll understand why this place makes me truly happy.

Upset

"And that I've met the most wonderful man in the world."

In a letter home to Frank, Sandra said: "I don't want to be cruel, but I'd better spell it out.

"I love Baks — it's a love much stronger than anything I've ever imagined.

"You knew you had lost me the first morning I saw Baks riding across the beach. I've got the chance of real happiness and I'm taking it."

Figure 3.   Monochrome inside section of the *Sun's* lead story for Monday 7 February 1994, giving the woman's version of events.

overall organisation of the story gelling around it as it informed the rest of the narrative. In providing the story with its centrally unifying thread, the combination of main headline, subsidiary headline and lead paragraph asserted the key interpretative cue for the reader.

In basic form this is all that is needed to be known about the narrative, which was in effect brought to closure by its initiating elements. At the same time, these elements also staked out the grounds on which the stereotyping would proceed in the remainder of the story. There are various ways in which this operated. To begin with, the first phrase in the primary juxtaposition of words in the banner headline – "Mud-Hut Rat" – related to the usual colloquial expression "love rat" often used in the *Sun* at this time (and subsequently) in its stories of celebrity sex and the extra-marital affairs of famous people, as for example with the English rugby player Will Carling. It could be argued that the familiarity of the phrase at the time meant that there was no need to use the word "love" in association with it, but dropping the first half of this diametrically contrasting term can also be seen as having supported the racially-informed core of the narrative. If the expression "love rat" is usually used in a metaphorical sense, the association with "mud huts" re-established some of the literal meaning of the epithet "rat", in that vermin are to be expected in rudimentary or "primitive" conditions, conditions that are stereotypically associated with "native life" in sub-Saharan Africa. These were made abundantly clear as the story unfolded. The husband in the story was quoted as saying: "She just didn't seem to care that he [the 'love rat'] lived in a horrible mud hut with no loo and just a charcoal fire to cook on". The point was then given further emphasis: "I couldn't believe that my wife, who always loved shopping and money, was going off to live in virtual squalor. They sleep on the floor over there. Hygiene is virtually non-existent". The woman herself, Sandra Anderson, was also quoted as saying that she was happy despite her new home having no running water and the toilet consisting of "an open cesspit in the garden", but this new-found happiness was played down in contrast to her steep descent from clean, respectable, English suburbia to "mud-hut squalor".

In the lead headline, the opposed categories of "rat" and "wife" were linked by the verb "stole". This had a pivotal position in the composition of the opening headline. It imparted a sense of activeness to the transition from wife to mistress, from responsible mother to sex-crazed concubine, although with blame being attributed to the "thief", Sagnia Bakary, the self-styled African prince. The transition-as-descent theme that was central to the racist stereotyping of the story was buttressed at the outset by the secondary oppositions in the lead paragraph between "businessman" and "native", and even more strongly in the second paragraph between "hubby Frank" and "black hunk". These oppositions were maintained throughout the story, as further detail made clear that "hubby Frank" (the term of endearment giving emphasis to his assigned position as the wronged party) was a financially-secure and dedicated owner of a landscaping enterprise in Leominster. The landscaped garden he had presumably created at his large Herefordshire home would have been utterly at odds with a mud hut and small attachment of land containing a "hole-in-the-ground" loo. Such oppositions, and the attribution of blame for what had happened, need to be understood in relation to a further dimension of the discourse schema. This is concerned with the sourcing and sequencing of citation in the narrative.

There was more or less an equality of treatment in the number of quotations attributed to husband and wife in the story. Roughly nine column inches were given over to statements from each of them. The equilibrium this appeared to create across the opposed "voices" of each party was clearly undermined by their narrative sequencing. All the quotes from Sandra Anderson were contained in the supplementary section on page four. Narrative priority and pre-eminence was given to the husband rather than the adulterous wife who had "dumped" him after 22 years of marriage. It was his side of the story that came first. Its sequencing not only gave it greater accreditation but also provided an interpretative frame through which the woman's statements were cited and set up to be assessed. The apparent equilibrium between the protagonists' "voices" in the story was subverted even more by the glaring absence of anything ascribed to Sagnia Bakary. His side of the story was ignored completely, with the implication that he was not worth consulting or, worse, not worthy of being consulted. The news story condemned him to narrative silence. The "voices" in the story were thus graded according to gender and ethnicity in the following way:

- *Frank's (white male) side of the story.* This followed directly from, and was directly implicated in, the nucleus of the story on page one. It was reinforced by further citation on page five (see Figure 2). His was the first and last "voice" heard in the story.
- *Sandra's (white female) side of the story.* This was introduced only on an inside page (see Figure 3) and so sandwiched in between what her husband had to say. It was also undercut by the thematic structure of the news narrative as a whole.
- *Sagnia's (black male) side of the story.* This was entirely missing. The narrative denied him any focalised viewpoint and rendered him, from the story's perspective, speechless. Instead, and in contrast to the two white protagonists, he was racially labelled as the "black hunk" who "stole" someone out of a state of holy matrimony.

Princely contrasts

As Bakary was neither visually nor vocally given presence in the article, he was discussed and so known about only through quotations from the two other protagonists and through the story as a whole put together by the reporter. The quantity of statements from the white protagonists in this triangle of relationships was also rendered insignificant in light of the quality of what they said and how this was treated. The husband's commentary and evaluation was wholly negative throughout. This surrounded the largely positive commentary and evaluation of the ex-wife. It also made suspect the acknowledgement she offered of her drastic loss of material security and the comforts of suburban life in England, along with her expression of regret over leaving her two sons. At the third point of the triangle, the silence attached to the black person's participation in the story appealed only to speculation and fancy, stereotype and myth, markers of which were set down from the outset in the way he was identified and labelled. As well as being described as a "mud-hut rat" who lived in "virtual squalor", the "black hunk" attribution drew directly on the racially stereotypical associations of black men with rampant libidos and an aggressive, insatiable sexuality. Throughout the story, a continual equation was made between, on the one hand, the exotic "sex in the sand" (the other kind of "riding lessons" implied in the narrative) and the "primitive" material conditions in which it occurred, and on the other, between wanton lubricity and lack of moral scruples (Bakary was said to be "out for what he can get", both from "hubby Frank" as well as his now ex-wife). These were all part of the thematic pattern of contrasts in the story, which also included that set up between erotic love and motherly love (Sandra's sons were said to be "stunned by their mum's departure" for a "shack" in "the middle of the Gambian bush"). The symbolic conjunction between sexual passion and racial atavism was then linked immediately to the price paid for this passion – the loss of modern civilisation.

The loss was indicated right from the start by the first-sentence description of Bakary as a "native". This is a term that comes laden with stereotypical associations, the term "black native" even more so. The interpretative cues contained in such associations are always prescriptive for potential readings. In this case, the term "native" carries highly condensed notions of social backwardness and racial inferiority. These were first crystallised and widely distributed during the period of "high" imperialism and colonialism when Britannia ruled the waves and much else besides. Those who live in the little England of the shires do not of course belong to the category "native". We would only refer to the "natives of Leominster" in an ironic or facetious sense, and certainly not in the same sense associated with Gambia or most other African nations. "Natives" are always other people, never "us". The term is an ideological device for distancing "us" from "them" and designating "them" as the primitive Other, as in the case of this tribal African prince. The term is self-validating: it confirms "us" in "our" position of civilised order, economic prosperity and technological advance. Here is where the intertextual relevance of the other front-page story in this edition of The *Sun* becomes abundantly clear (see Figure 1). To the left of the main story and immediately adjacent to it was a story about another prince, but not an African one.

The story concerned a real prince, a *bona fide* prince who is linked by blood to a long line of aristocratic breeding. The juxtaposition may appear quite fortuitous, but it clearly set up certain ideological relations across the two stories, particularly as their being placed side by side invited readers to attend to one immediately following the other. These relations were based around a further set of binary contrasts. The story about Prince Charles concerned the occasion in Australia when a student fired two shots from a starting pistol while the heir to the British throne was presiding over an awards ceremony. The English prince was described as reacting with measured dignity and calm, with the *sang froid* befitting a member of the nobility. The "ice-cool" demeanour he maintained in the face of this apparent attack was attributed to his "royal blue blood". He was quoted as saying: "A thousand years of breeding have gone into this, you know". In this way "our" prince, a royal emissary in a former colony that was once part of the glorious British Empire, was positioned as diametrically opposite in character and disposition to the African prince in the lead story. While the former was described as behaving with impeccable "good breeding", the latter was shown as hedonistic, unscrupulous and dishonourable. "Stealing" someone's wife and committing adultery could of course have been constructed as parallel narratives for both princes, but exactly the opposite ideological "effect" was achieved. There are Princes and princes, and what the putative difference symbolises is a long-established and enduring racial superiority.

From hell to paradise

There is another side to this stereotypical construction. To see it we need to return to the statements made by the "runaway mum". While these were set up to be interpreted through the negative frame already established in the accusatory statements made by her husband, Sandra (unlike her new lover) was given considerable space to explain the reasons for her precipitous shift from English suburbia to African bush. She does this through a further set of contrasts between her old life of marital misery and her new life of extra-marital bliss: "I've never really been happy before but this is like paradise on earth".

Sandra's declaration was prefaced by a description of her "stirring a pot on an open fire outside the shack she now calls home". The pejorative description and the direct quotation may seem to run counter to each other, with the weight of evidence falling on the extent to which Sandra had socially descended, but in the caption to an inside photograph image, she was also cited as saying that "life was 'hell' before she quit". The image showed her with her arm raised, as if in self-defence. It is unclear whether this is connected with the caption, but it is absolutely clear that she viewed her transition as moving from "hell" to "paradise" in one fell swoop. What she had lost in the life she left behind was of little consequence compared with what she had gained in the life she was now entered upon. Whereas her husband "took me for granted and kept telling me I was worthless", Baks "treated me so well, was so courteous and a real gentleman". She was said to "feel like a princess". A "princess in paradise" may not be expected to cook with a single pot on an open fire, never mind shit into "an open cesspit in the garden", but the prevailing reference was to how she felt and to her newfound fulfilment and happiness.

The disparity was given especial attention in the secondary headline on page four: "Loo Is A Hole In Ground But I've Found Paradise". The theme of transition-as-descent was reversed. A hole-in-the-ground toilet may have sounded more like paradise lost than paradise gained, and this was clearly the gloss put upon affairs by the jilted husband. Despite being framed by the sequencing of their two "voices", Sandra's emphasis on her feelings of love and satisfaction posited indubitable gain rather than loss. The theme thus changed to transition-as-ascent, from "hell" to "paradise", in a way that suggests a different source of appeal in the parable, one perhaps especially felt by women who were "taken for granted" or, worse, made to feel "worthless" by their partners. The appeal was at once emotional and sexual, deriving from the respect and courtesy accorded to her by her new lover, and from the sexual passion she was enjoying for the first time in her life – "Baks is a brilliant lover"; he "makes me feel like a real woman". Sandra coyly mentioned losing weight because of eating well and "all the exercise I'm getting, if you know what I mean". She was "totally happy for the first time". Again, the contrast was with her previous love of "shopping and money", implying that consumerist investments and chasing after happiness in commodities were poor substitutes for being made to feel "like a real woman".

The contrast is a commonplace one in popular culture. Given that in this case it was struck between a simple fulfilling life in the sun and an empty, unsatisfying suburban lifestyle worn down by mortgage worries, humdrum routine and the weight of middle age that two grown-up sons served to confirm, it is no surprise that Sandra compared what had happened with the narrative of the film *Shirley Valentine*, released four years earlier and starring Pauline Collins. So too did Frank, but his reference was to the self-serving flattery of Sagnia Bakary (his counterpart in the film being Costas, Shirley's Greek lover, played by Tom Conti). Frank regarded his ex-wife as having "lost all sense of reality because of the attention Bakary gave her". That is why for him it was "just like a scene from the movie *Shirley Valentine*". He contrasted this with his own situation, as "her husband back home, trying to pick up the pieces". His ex-wife clearly invested a different set of feelings in the comparison, and she also compared her affair with *Out of Africa*, the 1985 Oscar-winning film starring Meryl Streep and Robert Redford. This was based on the passionate love affair in Kenya between Karen Blixen (1885–1962) and Denys Finch Hatton (1887–1931), big-game safari hunter and son of the Earl of Winchilsea. Sandra considered her love affair as "like a mix of *Shirley Valentine* and *Out of Africa* – with more romance". Such analogies in quotations from participant sources in news narratives show how much films provide significant reference points in everyday life, regardless of whether they denote aspects of similarity or dissimilarity. In the story, they clearly denoted both. For Frank, the comparison was with loss of reality, reinforcing the notion of film as fiction, offering make-believe worlds that diverge from the necessary actualities of ordinary social life – in this case, romance in the negative sense. Sandra, by contrast, used the term "romance" in a positive way; her own new life resembled a love story in the cinema but was superior because it provided even "more romance". Her sense of romance was nevertheless rooted firmly in cinematic references: "I've always dreamed of being whisked away in the sunshine by a man on a horse and now it's happened". Romance and reality had converged.

Comparisons between films and events in people's personal lives hinge around these ambiguities of meaning and value, switching between film as cinematic illusion and film as naturalist representation, film as unreal and film as capturing the dramatic reality of interpersonal relationships and the collision of different needs and imperatives, different hopes and desires, and different ways of seeing and accounting for what has happened. So, for example, Frank confined his comparison to *Shirley Valentine*, not because it involves the return of a somewhat chastened wife (Frank declared he would not take her back because of fear of HIV/AIDS) but because it depicts a sexually opportunist, morally unscrupulous, foreign lover. Similarly, Sandra's reference to *Out of Africa* spoke to her own situation in at least two ways. Karen Blixen/Isak Dinesen wrote passionately and without sentimentality of the Kikuyu and her life in the Ngong Hills of Kenya in her autobiography *Out of Africa* (Blixen 1971), but never attained the same objectivity when writing about her fabled lover, Finch Hatton, who she depicted as a model of male perfection. "He is always presented by her as a god, who swoops from the sky in his little aeroplane bearing happiness" and possessing "a powerful, wide-ranging mind and natural authority" (Amory 1981; see also Trzebinski 1977; Wheeler 2006).[4] The parallel in the heroic way Sandra portrays her new lover is clear, but there is another parallel in the abandonment not only of life in civilised Europe but also in Sandra's rejection of bourgeois respectability. Karen Blixen wrote to her Aunt Bess (Mary Bess Westenholz, 1857–1947) that "there is so much in life to love, so much to live for, that to me there is something blasphemous about this monopoly of love and cooperation between human beings by marriage and family life" (Dinesen 1981, 394). Such monopoly relates to bourgeois standards and ideals, and it is these Sandra has turned her back on.

Populist primitivism

It could be said that this tabloid news story also dealt with this drama and the divergent paths that had split open a longstanding marriage, but – in line with the *Sun's* general "conservative articulation of de-subordinate impulses" – it did not question or challenge the social conventions regarding marriage and family life, particularly as they affect women (McGuigan 1992, 185; see also Miliband 1978). Its treatment of the triadic set of relationships in the story worked within the bounds of normality and, even more significantly, through the reproduction of various racial myths and stereotypes.[5] The myths and stereotypes were both social and sexual. All the details surrounding the polar opposition between the comfort and security of suburban England and the crude living arrangements in the Gambian bush played on the stereotypical civilised/primitive divide that grew up in the later nineteenth century and is an enduring legacy of Victorian racism and imperialism. In contrast to earlier distinctions, this divide has operated to anachronistically position Africa and African people over against Europe and Europeans and to symbolically place them on an evolutionist scale of social development and progress, with the former representing backwardness and stagnation and the latter enterprise, achievement and innovation. The many diverse ways of life in the African continent were long thought of as those of "people without history". This belief found its latter-day counterpart in Sagnia Bakary's "person without voice" – his routine exclusion from the accounts that count.

The unequal axis of the imperial relation was reproduced in the confinement of narrative voices to a male/female dyad that consolidated the sense of white priority and superiority. The opposition of female and male viewpoints set up by the story was that between romantic happiness and sexual fulfilment, and suburban prosperity and conjugal obligations. This was mapped onto the civilised/primitive dichotomy in such a way that maleness was made to uphold a sense of adhering to reality and femaleness a sense of losing touch with reality. The "normal" husband was also counterposed to the "wayward" wife and "native" hunk in such a way as to reproduce the old notion of "going native", making that precipitous leap across the civilised/primitive divide. If that leap has usually created fears and anxieties in the bourgeois breast, these have been accompanied by their shadow fears and anxieties, coalescing around the doubt that civilised life may be deficient in certain ways, and lacking in something vital, such as adventure, passion, risk. This is acknowledged in the story, for Sandra was allowed to contrast the previous deficiencies in her life with her then current sexual and romantic happiness. To attain such happiness, she had been willing to sacrifice her settled nuclear family set-up and turn her back on the past. Despite the basic material conditions of her new life (albeit stereotypically portrayed), she had discovered and attained what was previously absent in her life.

The *Sun*'s story did not openly side with either the man or the woman, but it did give priority to the man's account and allowed it normatively to mediate and position the woman's account. The two accounts did not count in the same way. Their inclusion invited alternative readings but at the same time rendered one less compelling in the stakes of credibility, never mind less commanding in the scales of responsibility. The power of the story's rhetorical organisation is that it appeared to offer equal space to both accounts while ensuring that the conventional white male viewpoint prevailed. In doing this, it depended ideologically on a white/black male contrast that drew implicitly on some of the key stereotypical notions of biological racism. The problem of the late-twentieth century was still the problem of the colour line, and the racism at the core of that problem continued to be infused with sexual apprehensions and anxieties. "From New Orleans to New Guinea, from Barbados to Bulawayo, from Kimberley to Kuala Lumpur, the quintessential taboo to be explained is the white man's formal objection to intimacy between black men and white women" (Hyam 1992, 203).[6] Such a taboo no longer formally exists and cannot be justified on any official grounds, but that does not mean that the objection, or the white male insecurities and fears on which it rests, no longer apply. News stories like that of the *Sun*, play on and help perpetuate, in however covert or attenuated a fashion, mythical notions not only of black men having larger penises than white men, but also having a higher sex drive and greater sexual staying power. Along with this erotic privilege has been a compensating, but equally mythical, notion of black racial inferiority on the grounds of lower intelligence, reduced powers of rationality, hedonistic impulses and lack of restraint, discipline and ambition. Sexual prejudices are often closely interwoven with racial antagonisms. Open expression of such antagonisms in the popular press of the early 1990s was less acceptable than it had previously been, but obviously this did not prevent their ideological rationale continuing to be given clear articulation. Myths that help ground nationalist legitimacy and ensure social reproduction often show remarkable persistence. This again is where cross-narrative interaction is important.

All newspapers are mosaics of narrative and representation whose different elements appear formally unrelated to each other, yet at the same time they are composed both on single pages and as a whole, and subject to various editorial decisions that are driven by particular news values and broader commercial imperatives. This may mean that interpreting the *Sun*'s advert for its Snakes and Ladders scratch-card game, which was placed immediately above the Mud-Hut Rat story in the top half of the front page, as bearing sexual metaphors and allusions to the rungs of civilisational progress, is to find evidence of intertextual relations that would hardly register with the majority of its readers. This is not the case with the two lead stories. Both were about princes, of alleged or proven royal descent, and so directly invited comparative assessment. Sandra Anderson referred to Sagnia Bakary as "a real gentleman", yet the strategic contrasts and oppositions in the narrative as a whole seemed to support retention of the view, developed from the mid-nineteenth century, that white skin was "an essential mark of a gentleman" and that "even 'a self-improved Negro' could not rise to the elevated status of a gentleman" (Lorimer 1978, 15). The paradise-from-hell trajectory ran in a contradictory direction to the theme of downward social mobility, and so may have lent support to the claim that the "tribal prince" was indeed "a real gentleman", but the possibility of this was seriously weakened by the *Sun*'s reminder of what real gentlemanly status entailed – a thousand years of all-white racial breeding, and the aristocratic attributes of calm dignity and "natural authority" that go with this. These could not be shown to be as clearly apparent in the heartbroken businessman/husband. The necessary comparison lay readily to hand in the Prince Charles story. For once, it was his good repute rather than his risible foibles that was being foregrounded in Britain's best-selling newspaper.

Primitivism has always played fear and fascination ambivalently off against each other, whether in high cultural modernism or popular music and dance, with the appeal being either to a temporary or a more durable reaction against conventional social values. The *Sun* story offered both these dimensions of primitivism and so allowed its readers to ask projective "what if" questions, but not in the end at the expense of a balanced choice of sympathy for the two antagonists. The man's situation was given preferential treatment as heartbreak and betrayal, and the women's exploits were seen through a white erotic imaginary. This in turn revolved around the lack of established English social norms that the narrative served to endorse. Invoking an ingrained sense of hierarchical ethnic classification, the story took perceived sexual infraction as the chief vehicle for re-establishing their legitimacy. In doing so, this late-twentieth-century sample of populist primitivism demonstrated the resilience of racial stereotypes that, despite their imperial and colonial origins, seemed to retain the strength of their pernicious notions in a new historical context. It showed how such stereotypes can still be made to "fit the moment" when black/white interethnic relations are no longer the sexual taboo they have previously been. The primitive black stereotype has always been an ideological construct, and the outcome remains the same. Perpetuating the myth of the primitive black Other relies on the continuance of racist images that not only demean its stereotyped objects but also relegate them to silence, and symbolically exclude them from the order of civilised society.

Notes

1. On stereotypes, see Pickering (2001, 2004a, 2004b and 2007); see also Allport (1954), Bhabha (1997, chapter 3) and Hinton (2000).
2. The analytical method on which this article is loosely based is set out in Deacon et al. (2007, chapters 7 and 8).
3. See Chippindale and Horrie (1990) for a general account of the development of the *Sun*'s tabloid journalism.
4. Finch Hatton took up flying in 1929 and bought a Gypsy Moth airplane a year later. It was in this plane that he crashed fatally in 1931. As Christopher Ondaatje (2006) noted in a review of her book, Sara Wheeler "silently corrects" Robert Redford's "grossly inaccurate portrait of Finch Hatton" in the film. Isak Dinesen was the pen name of Karen Blixen.
5. This article focuses on the ideological consequences of these myths and stereotypes rather than the extent to which the content of the story did or did not correspond with the events. Any embroidery of the facts of the case is not strictly relevant to this primary analytical focus.
6. On sexual relations between white and black men and women in North America in the postwar period, see Hernton (1970) and Day (1974).

References

Allport, G. 1954. *The nature of prejudice.* Cambridge, MA: Addison Wesley.
Amory, M. 1981. The African Queen, review of Dinesen 1981. *Sunday Times*, 13 September.
Bhabha, H. 1997. *The location of culture.* London: Routledge.
Blixen, K. 1971/1937. *Out of Africa.* London: Jonathan Cape.
Chippindale, P., and C. Horrie.. 1990. *Stick it up your punter! The rise and fall of the Sun.* London: Heinemann.
Day, B. 1974. *Sexual life between blacks and whites.* London: Collins.
Deacon, D., M. Pickering, P. Golding, and G. Murdock. 2007. *Researching communications: A practical guide to methods in media and cultural analysis*, 2nd edition. London: Hodder Arnold.
Dinesen, I. 1981. *Letters from Africa 1914–1931.* London: Weidenfeld and Nicolson.
Hernton, C. 1970. *Sex and racism.* London: Paladin.
Hinton, P. 2000. *Stereotypes, cognition and culture.* Hove: Psychology Press.
Hyam, R. 1992. *Empire and sexuality.* Manchester: Manchester University Press.
Lorimer, D. 1978. *Colour, class and the Victorians.* Leicester: Leicester University Press.
McGuigan, J. 1992. *Cultural populism.* London: Routledge.
Miliband, R. 1978. A state of de-subordination. *British Journal of Sociology* 29, no. 4.
Ondaatje, C. 2006. Animal passion flies high above the Serengeti. *Times Higher*, 7 April.
Pickering, M. 2001. *Stereotyping: The politics of representation.* Basingstoke: Palgrave Macmillan.
———. 2004a. The inescapably social concept of stereotyping. In *The power and persistence of stereotyping – O poder e a persistência dos estereótipos*, ed. A. Barker, 21–32. Aveiro: Universidade de Aveiro.
———. 2004b. Racial stereotypes. In *Social identity: Multidisciplinary approaches*, ed. G. Taylor and S. Spencer, 91–106. London: Routledge.
———. 2007. Stereotypes and stereotyping. In *Blackwell encyclopedia of sociology*, ed. G. Ritzer. 10 vols. Vol. 10, 4773–8. Oxford: Blackwell.
Trzebinski, E. 1977. *Silence will speak: A study of the life of Denys Finch Hatton and his relationship with Karen Blixen.* London: Heineman.
Wheeler, S. 2006. *Too close to the Sun: The life and times of Denys Finch Hatton.* London: Jonathan Cape.

"The road to the lesbian nation is not an easy one": "us" and "them" in *Diva* magazine

Georgina Turner

The present paper discusses *Diva*, Britain's only mainstream lesbian magazine. Using critical discourse analysis, the article explores *Diva*'s importance to its readers and the pertinence of critical discourse analysis techniques to analysing the magazine. Looking at six consecutive issues, the study focuses on a close textual analysis, backed up by content analysis, of how the groups "us" and "them" are constructed. The paper concludes that the magazine's use of these categories in ways that bemoan yet bolster the distance between the two reflects *Diva*'s position as the voice of an "oppressed group".

Introduction

This paper forms part of an ongoing study addressing the (re)production of lesbian identity in *Diva* magazine. Since 1994, *Diva* has been the United Kingdom's only mainstream lesbian magazine, whose stated purpose is "to entertain and inform its readers about issues and events of importance to lesbian women, to provide a forum for discussion with the lesbian communities, and to encourage lesbians and bi women to feel happy and positive about their sexuality".[1] It is sold monthly and is Europe's best-selling lesbian magazine.

Despite the prevalence of work addressing mainstream women's magazines as sites at which *heterosexual* womanhood is constructed and construed (for example, Kim and Ward 2004; McCracken 1993; Ferguson 1983), and more recently proliferating studies involving masculinity and men's magazines (for example, Benwell 2003; Crewe 2003; Boni 2002), work analysing *in-group* media representations of lesbians and lesbian identity is limited. Driver (2007) includes *Diva* among other hetero-publications and homo-publications in her study of young lesbians and popular culture, but focuses very specifically on teen consumption and comparisons between the ways in which each magazine is negotiated. Wong and Zhang's (2001) work on Taiwan's *G&L Magazine* addresses the construction of an imagined community of "*Tóngzhìmen*" (comrades). Their textual observations are aimed at highlighting the style in which *G&L* manages its community of readers as the Tóngzhì, rather than addressing the ways in which broader gay/lesbian identities are constructed. Livia (2002) looks at French magazine *Lesbia*, focusing on how the readers, with steering from editors, manage inclusion and exclusion through the personal adverts.

Her key concern is with how they (re)produce an environment of anti-masculine hostility. No work (that I have found) takes as its focus the ways in which the writers and editors of a lesbian magazine construct and police in-group identity as a multi-faceted project.

This seems an extraordinary omission given the powerful nature of the media in general, and the highly persuasive nature of specialist magazines in particular, which are often considered an authoritative mouthpiece by and for the people they "represent" (Peterson 1964). *Diva* makes a particularly powerful case to consider: the goals listed in its purpose statement are highly agenda-setting (what is important to lesbian women?, what are safe/important topics for discussion?, and which communities or parts of communities can join in?); the magazine has a 14-year standing as the United Kingdom's only mainstream lesbian magazine, and is increasingly able to command an audience with leading lesbian icons (Sharon Stone, the cast of hit American drama *The L Word* and gay-press-shy Ellen Degeneres all featured in 2007). With an estimated readership of 100,000,[2] the magazine offers a link between (potentially isolated) individuals and a significant community of women. Gillian Rodgerson, editor between 1997 and 2004, says that the magazine sees itself as a first point of contact for lesbians and an "information tool".[3] Numerous letters from readers throughout the magazine's history – "*Diva* has changed my life", "A lifeline to my gay world", "Informed me of all the different aspects of gay culture" (to quote just a few) – suggest that women, particularly young or "new" lesbians, turn to *Diva* to learn about their sexual identity. It is a space in which readers can read *as lesbians* (Wilton 1995) and find cultural commentary where mainstream women's magazines ignore or marginalise them (Ballaster et al. 1991). No claims are made as to the homogeneity of readers, nor their use of the magazine – indeed, as Livia (2002) points out, we must include in any community of readers those who resist the magazine's values. This does nothing, however, to dull *Diva*'s potential influence.

Critical discourse analysis

Critical discourse analysis (CDA) is a functionalist approach to discourse that posits language use as a social practice; a given discursive event shares a dialectical relationship with its situational, institutional and social contexts (Fairclough and Wodak 1997), simultaneously *reflecting* the realities of the social world and helping to *compose* that reality (Phillips and Jorgensen 2002). CDA aims, then, to link linguistic analysis to social analysis (Wood and Kroger 2000) in order to make transparent discourse's role in (re)producing social life. Work may focus variously on cognition, context and critical linguistics, but combines, or aims to combine, three levels of analysis: text, discourse practice and socio-cultural practice (Fairclough 1995).

Textual analysis works from the minutiae of lexicon, syntax and grammar up to the way a text is organised and structured. What the analyst is looking at, essentially, are the features of the text that make it read a certain way. A reading of the text informed by an understanding of the discourse practices at work in and on a text – the conventions of the organisation generating it, and the social conditions shaping the way readers decode the text – follows. Finally, the ideas produced by these two levels of analysis are critiqued in light of the socio-cultural context of which the discursive event is part (Fairclough 1995). That is, the analyst should explore and explain their interpretation of the text by reference to the social reality it constitutes and construes.

A primary concern in CDA is unequal power relations, and the victims of the discriminatory discourses that those imbalances produce. CDA work is usually motivated by a desire to scrutinise and expose elite ideologies at work in discourse, point out the relationship between this and the social conditions they (re)create, and effect change as a result. This, clearly, is not research of that kind. It is fruitful nonetheless, I would argue, to approach *Diva* from a CDA perspective.

Firstly, as suggested above, *Diva* is potentially a very persuasive magazine. Given its unique visibility and standing in what I will carefully call, for need of brevity and while acknowledging its insufficiency as a concept, the lesbian community, *Diva* is exceptionally well placed to "organise the multitude of beliefs about what is the case, good or bad, right or wrong, *for [members of a group]*" (van Dijk 1998, 8; emphasis in original). That is, the magazine plays a prominent ideological role. Secondly, CDA is useful because of the rarity of approaching an in-group text in this manner, asking the same questions, examining the same relationships, but from within, aimed not at liberating the victims but at understanding how the same uneven social relations are brought to bear on in-group texts and the changes that understanding might effect. Essentially, the present article employs CDA to take a critical interest in a minority discourse, rather than a discourse *about minorities*.

Diva in its social context

The sample used here comes from 2002–2003, a period during which lesbians, as part of the wider group "homosexuals", were still battling for basic equality, let alone progressive rights. The ban on gays in the military had not long been lifted; the repeal of Section 28[4] had yet to happen. The battle for equality in the workplace was new-born compared with these fights; same-sex partnership legislation similarly infantile. Public feeling was perhaps improving thanks to the increased visibility of homosexuality in mainstream media, but this visibility brought with it its own problems. Months before the start of the sample, the General Teaching Council issued a Draft Professional Code, including a clause requiring teachers to respect differences of sexual orientation. The clause was the result of lobbying from Stonewall over homophobic bullying in schools. It was received badly (and loudly) by the Christian Institute, while *Mail on Sunday* columnist Peter Hitchens described it as a "nasty development" and a "new censorship".[5] Neither Hitchens', nor the Christian right's, attitudes to homosexuality need further explication here, but both point to a mainstream discourse littered with negative, often confrontational, references to homosexuality. The way in which *Diva* constructs in-group and out-group identities – who are "we", who are "they" and how do we feel about each other? – in this context is therefore extremely pertinent.

Data and method

The paper focuses on six consecutive editions of *Diva*, beginning in August 2002 and ending in January 2003, a spell that straddles a redesign and change of strapline (discussed below). Following the thoughts of McLoughlin (2000) and Eggins and Iedema (1997) on germane magazine content, the sample includes editor's letters ($n = 6$), news reports ($n = 12$), interviews ($n = 12$), features ($n = 20$), horoscopes ($n = 6$) and front covers ($n = 6$), although not all of these genres feature in the extracts used here.

The first stage of the research was a quantitative content analysis of the entire sample, noting the signifiers for women and correlations between the use of particular nouns (e.g. "dyke") and certain topics (e.g. "activism"). Although only speculative inferences can be made by describing these "manifest features" of the text (Berelson 1971), the patterns described in naming women (readers, interviewees, others) allow us to see beyond individual examples and sketch the contours of the landscape as a whole. It is with reference to this map that the more hermeneutic discourse analytic findings are strengthened and contextualised (Winston 1990).

Each article was then subjected to (critical) discourse analytic readings, informed largely by Fairclough's (1989, 92–93) and Wood and Kroger's (2000, 91–95) guidelines for textual analysis (Richardson [2006] includes an excellent chapter on textual analysis for those less familiar with a CDA approach). The primary interest, in asking these questions about lexicalisation, transitivity, text structure, and so forth, was in the construction of the group "us" and the corresponding group "them".

Analysis

The analysis is divided into two parts. The first addresses the construction of a lesbian world bound by concepts of "us" and "them". The second looks at how "they" are constructed, and tensions implied between these groups.

Lesbianism: the walled garden

The lesbian identity constructed in *Diva* is one heavily dependent on boundaries; some erected by the in-group to maintain the "us-ness" of "us", and some that isolate "us" from "them": heterosexual society. The invisible line that separates the two worlds is made frequently visible by, for example, references to couples, which become the more formal "same-sex couples" in news articles relating to legislation (and thus the outside world) whereas they had been "girl couples", "dykes and their ladies" and "me and the missus" elsewhere.

Keeping us "us"

The drawing of boundaries around (minority) groups is an important part of turning those imagined communities into something tangible for their members to identify with; a means of self-definition and group definition (Martin 1996; Eves 2004). In the sample, readers are thoroughly "desocialised" (Eggins and Iedema 1997) – that is, notions of race, economic/ class status, ethnicity and education are suppressed in order to create a single, recognisable in-group identity centred on sexual identity.

> *Extract 1*
> One strange night, not so long ago, I saw a dyke struggling along the street, weighed down by the biggest cauldron of soup I'd ever seen. Behind her, another dyke dragged a trailer containing a huge pot of vegetable curry.[6]

In Extract 1, the writer chooses to identify the women she saw as "dykes" immediately. Since soup and curry are unlikely markers of lesbian identity, this entails that there are other things available to group members that enable them to spot one another. Exactly what these are is not made explicit, but the reader is positioned as someone to whom these spotting devices are also available; the women's immediate identification as dykes is not in anyway problematic. It is in the knowing and demonstrating of these signifiers, then, that the individual's claim on in-group identity is confirmed – or denied.

> *Extract 2*
> "Okay Gemma. Madge or Kylie?"
> "Arghh ... definitely Kylie – everybody's going to hate me, but I don't care!"

"Sex or food?" "Food and sex!"
"Trousers or skirts?" "Trousers!"
"And, finally – Peggy or Pat?" "Pat!"
Right. That's our Gemma then.[7]

Here we see the process of negotiating in-group status explicitly played out. There are "right" and "wrong" answers – after deliberating over her reply, interviewee Gemma Hayes acknowledges that choosing Kylie is "wrong" and dissentient. But her lack of hesitation and emphatic(!) replies to the other questions signals a feeling that they are "right" – indeed, her responses almost suggest an "of course". The interviewer also confirms her correctness in the finishing line, her summation ("Right") suggesting an appropriateness to Hayes's answers that is confirmed in the claiming of Hayes as "ours".

Extract 3
Several of the episodes focus on unusual sexual proclivities … In one, we see Anna try to understand Rockbitch, an all-girl metal band whose members practise a self-conceived form of lesbian-esque witchcraft. That is, when they're not shagging strange men in Amsterdam's porn cinemas.[8]

By contrast, in Extract 3 we can see the careful management of what – or who is not –"us". Despite a shift from the strapline "Lesbian life and style" to the more fluid "For the lesbian in you" in November 2002 (the middle of the sample), *Diva* is not somewhere that bisexual women see themselves – at least not in preferential terms. The use of the suffix *-esque* frames Rockbitch's bisexuality as a pseudo-sexuality, something resembling (but perhaps something less than, or inferior to) lesbianism, although not closely enough that lesbian Anna Nolan can understand it without some effort. There is also some ambiguity surrounding "self-conceived" – does it apply simply to the witchcraft, or the likening, however loosely, of bisexuality to lesbianism?

"They" don't like us

Although the in-group appears to depend on boundaries in order to maintain the category "us", it is also possible to read in the sample a feeling that the divide between "us" and "them" is one of "their" making, designed to sustain a heterosexist hierarchy.

Extract 4
It is no easy thing to give up the safety and privilege of a heterosexual life [. . .] Of course, the road to the lesbian nation is not an easy one. Many women gave the most heartbreaking accounts of what they had to lose along the way. But, for all the pain and sheer hard work, leaving heterosexuality for the lesbian life was, for most of them, an extraordinary and liberating journey.[9]

Here we see what is actually one of several references in the sample to "the lesbian nation" – elsewhere described, somewhat tongue in cheek, as "the ghetto" – standing in contrast to "the heterosexual world". In constructing lesbian and heterosexual life in spatial terms, they cease to be sexualities, which we might consider fluid character traits or expressions, and become more rigid places. They can thus never exist together; a person in one place is removed from the other. These places must be travelled to and from, and are separated, apparently, by a vast and difficult terrain. It is interesting that the arduousness of this journey is known – "of course" – to readers, despite the fact that they are addressed throughout the rest of the article as women who have never travelled from heterosexuality to "the lesbian nation". Perhaps it is not, then, the journey that is familiar, but the things that must be surrendered on departure. Heterosexuality is "safe" and "privileged" (and elsewhere "traditional" and "protected"), leaving lesbians unsafe and disadvantaged. The construction of lesbian identity as institutionally unprotected can also be seen in numerous allusions to the constant torment of lesbians by heterosexual society.

Extract 5
It was an NHS clinic which had never before provided fertility services to lesbians. So Jan and Sarah were not unduly surprised when they were turned away. What did surprise them was the reason they were given – the clinic claimed it had no sperm. A tad suspicious, they wondered whether this was a novel excuse for discrimination.[10]

The scene setting in Extract 5 ensures the reader is immediately aware that the clinic is part of an establishment: the National Health Service (NHS). It is presupposed that, in such a setting, prejudice towards lesbians is so common that it is the excuses (note the category shift from "reason") that change, rather than the treatment – the couple apparently expect to be told no, and we might read that their expectations are determined by the fact that the clinic is part of the NHS. "So" might just as likely share an anaphoric relationship with the "NHS-ness" of the clinic as it does with its service history, even if we cannot assume that the two go hand in hand. The physicality of "turned away" (as opposed to "turned down", or "refused", which are arguably equally available to the writer) recalls again this idea of spaces and denied entry and speaks to a reader who understands this as part of a catalogue of negative experiences. The readers' lived experience of these prejudices is often used, as in "a familiar feeling of discontentment ... being treated like shit at straight venues".[11]

Throughout the sample, lesbians' poor treatment at the hands of heterosexual society is constructed as intentional and malicious. While gay activism is spoken of as a necessary (and just) challenge, heterosexist actions and sentiments are "crusades" led by "heavy-handed" "militants".

Extract 6
Baroness Young was a tireless campaigner against equal rights for lesbians and gay men. Despite serious ill health, she dragged herself from her sickbed earlier this year in order to oppose a bill to allow adoption by unmarried couples [...] Her strategy for mobilising anti-gay feeling often depended on misinformation and scaremongering. During her crusade to keep the age of consent at 18 for gay men ... [...] She was defeated in her battle against the age of consent, but proved a more successful figurehead in the campaign to retain Section 28.[12]

Given the nature of obituaries, it is not surprising that they are generally written to mark the death of prominent lesbians, feminists and equal rights campaigners. Here, however, we have an obituary for staunch heterosexist Baroness Young, which has the feel of a victory dance to mark the demise of an old adversary. These terms are used here very deliberately, given the vivid war imagery with which the Conservative peer's unflinching campaign against gay equality is constructed. She appears as the figurehead of a crusade, strategising and mobilising her forces. Baroness Young is presented as the author of her campaign throughout; this is "her battle". It is interesting that her opposition is constructed as being against "equal rights for lesbians and gay men", rather than simply "gay rights". Her distaste for "equality", let alone what might sound like anything more progressive, perhaps suggests a far less reasonable person – an unreasonableness backed up by her illustratively-invoked willingness to disregard her own health.

Outside the walls: others

Having built these at times seemingly insurmountable walls, it is no surprise, really, to find *Diva*'s relationship with those on the other side apparently fraught with difficulty. Relations with bisexual women were touched upon briefly earlier and are likely to be the focus of future work, so the remainder of the analysis will focus on heterosexual women, and men, and their construction as "other".

Women featured in the magazine are treated overwhelmingly positively – according to the content analysis, all named subjects and interviewees are spoken of in glowing terms, often being treated to intensified adjectives like "incredibly charismatic" and "extremely talented". The talents of interviewees are routinely foregrounded and they are more often allowed to speak for themselves than be paraphrased.

However, heterosexual women rarely feature as the primary subject of articles, and where they appear as a group they are commonly disparaged as the cosseted beneficiaries of a society in which they can choose the safety of the traditional nuclear family. "They" are alternately scorned as the willing victims of patriarchy and despised for their comfort within it. Straight women remain very much the other: content analysis shows that gay women are more than twice as likely to be referred to as lesbians than as women, a label more often reserved for their heterosexual counterparts. In one article,[13] only "lesbians" and "heterosexual women" exist; the generic category "woman" is completely absent. Even on the topic of feminism, womanhood remains a contested area:

Extract 7
I'm so pleased to hear young women like the members of Le Tigre not only happily describing themselves as feminists, but also working actively to encourage other women. The last twenty years have seen bitter battles amongst women, and, it seems, especially amongst lesbians, over who gets to use the world "feminist" [...] "Feminist" came to be a dirty word for some women. "I'm not a feminist or anything, but ..." they'll say, going on to express a perfectly reasonable, and undoubtedly feminist, point of view. Who on earth do they think *is* a feminist? And it's not just straight girls using the word "feminist" as a euphemism for "lesbian" either.[14]

The first half of the extract contains several instances of "women" where the sexuality of those women is not made explicit. Given that the article is about feminism, we might reasonably infer that they speak of *all* women. Certainly "amongst women" suggests a general category reference, since "lesbians" are then picked out from within that. Then comes "some women", which clearly applies to another (at this point potentially overlapping) section of the more general "women". However, "some women" quickly becomes "they" (underlined). Now, "some women" and "they" both seem to point to the same group as "straight girls" – for two reasons. First, the appearance of "just", used as a synonym for "only", suggests a cataphoric relationship between "they" and "straight girls" – "And it's not *only* [those people] using ...". This construction only appears to make sense if "some women", "they" and "straight girls" are co-referential. Second, the writer asks a direct question of the reader, in which "they" are referred to and following which "straight girls" appears. The reader, then, cannot make sense of the question without hearing "they" as "women who are not us". It is interesting that, having established this divide between "us" and "them", the writer then downgrades heterosexual women to girls. This is not, of course, a category reference to juvenile females, but works perhaps to suggest immaturity and a scaling-down of intellectual capability. "*St*raight girls" also contains the kind of "spitting phonetics" that enable the speaker to insinuate disgust or disdain (Miller and Swift 1976).

Men do not feature highly in the sample, as might be expected in a lesbian lifestyle magazine. The ways in which they feature when they do appear, however, are incredibly interesting.

Gay men appear to be convenient allies in the political/public arenas: every news report in the sample relating to gay – as opposed to exclusively lesbian – issues includes lesbians and gay men. But in more socio-cultural contexts, my reading of *Diva* suggests a division between the two groups; content analysis showed that the magazine is eight times more likely to refer to women as "lesbian" than "gay", and this disassociation is evident in much talk about "gay" events.

Extract 8
Why a Dyke March the night before Pride? "It's an answer to the commercialism of Pride. We take no corporate money, only individual donations," Anne Pollock reported. "And it's an opportunity for dykes to practise leadership and organisational skills. Women don't have to fight to be heard".[15]

Pride, a supposedly shared event, is constructed here as an occasion that leaves dykes feeling sidelined and ignored. It appears they have to struggle to make their voices heard – above the men, we must conclude, for who else is involved? – and find limited opportunities to help coordinate/manage operations. Further, the use of *practise* suggests that these are not skills lesbians lack, but that their capabilities are ignored or suppressed by the "noisy" men. Other articles in the sample suggest that male dominance in planning events also limits lesbian enjoyment of the events themselves.

With this in mind, it is interesting that gatherings like Pride are often labelled queer – content analysis showed that *Diva* was 15 times more likely to use the label "lesbian" than "queer" for women. Its use invokes the distance between "us" and these events and, perhaps, queer politics, which were seen by some to construct an identity that ignored the different experience of lesbians and gay men (Martin 1996) using a strongly male referent.

Frequent references to the commercialisation of Pride events and the demise of "marches" and the rise of "parades" as changes unwanted by "us" but engineered by "them" help to manufacture a picture of gay men as having abandoned their political principles in the name of consumerism and an easier ride in the mainstream. They are often referred to as "gay boys" or "the boys", which suggests a lack of responsibility, and points to a group not to be taken too seriously.

Extract 9
It felt like we were probably the only dykes on the island. Our hotel was wall-to-wall gay boys. The swimming trunks, the late-night corridor bumpings and the soundtrack pumping out by the pool told us so. [...] Suffering from stereotype overdrive, I had expected our pool to be an OTT gay holiday sensation – drag queens, camp icons, fag hags and sailor boys liberally littering the poolside.[16]

The identifiers for "gay boys" are swimwear, public sexual encounters and music, and the categories to which gay men are allocated are largely effeminate and connote vanity and inanity. The use, then, of "dyke" is important – not only does the more casual term allow the writer the space and licence to heavily stereotype her male counterparts, but it sets up a stark contrast with the nature of the "gay boys" – "dyke" is more heavily associated with politics and activism in the sample than any other topic.

Heterosexual men are configured as a "known unknown"; a group that is estranged from us, and whose behaviours are often incompatible with "our" own, but that is simultaneously familiar. This can be seen particularly in their construction as lovers. In an article about previously heterosexual women who become lesbians, one interviewee refers to sex with men as "an alien, animal experience", which the writer transforms into "alien bodies of male partners".[17] Even as partners, men remain irreconcilably incongruous creatures – and yet at the same time their sexuality is apparently more than familiar. In an article about Mexican artist Frida Kahlo, the fact that both Kahlo and husband Diego Rivera enjoyed frequent extra-marital affairs is noted. Kahlo goes on to be described as being "devoted to" Rivera; he, by contrast, becomes "a monumental womaniser".[18] Heterosexual men are often constructed as "twisted guys" whose sex drive is indomitable and whose "prurient" interest in lesbians is a given.

There is one area of lesbian life, however, where men play an important role – although that role is constantly elided in *Diva*. While it is understandable that, in this context, the raising of a child might be discussed as a role for mother(s), men remain an absent presence even in the process of conceiving a child – referred to at one point as "grabbing spare swimmers".[19]

Extract 10
Until we live in a future where we all wear unisex silver jumpsuits, travel by personal jetpack and grow babies in pods, lesbians who are considering popping a sprog of their own will have to contend with the sticky subject of sperm. Getting hold of the stuff can be tricky enough, getting pregnant with it is often trickier still, and then, when you think your turkey-basting days are long gone, the source of those chromosomes can come back into your life in ways that you never expected.[20]

This extract comes from an article ostensibly aimed at providing the reader with information and advice about becoming a parent. The military metaphor in the headline – "Sperm wars" – however, reveals more about the nature of the author's argument. What she actually seems to take the reader through is a guide to the hows and the whys of negotiating the acquisition of sperm without the acquisition of the accompanying man. It is this tricky transaction that lesbians must "contend with". In paragraph two we are told, "for lesbians who have become – or want to become – parents via a donor, sperm has become the subject of some bitter fights". The rest of the article makes it clear, however, that the subject of these fights is in fact fathers wanting more involvement with, or access to, their children, and not the sperm they are reduced to by the writer.

Of course, there is a danger in using fatherhood discourse because of the implications of parental involvement and responsibility that the term "father" carries. By and large fathers are written out of the equation – "a sprog *of their own*" – and denied agency; lesbians "get hold of" sperm and get themselves pregnant. Fathers are euphemistically referred to as "the sticky subject of sperm" and "the source of those chromosomes" or "the guy who helped you out". Elsewhere, in an article about whether or not it is important for children to know their fathers, the writer avoids the word "father" by referring to "a [child's] right to know their full genetic heritage".[21] The word "father" comes in only when the relevant legislation is quoted. Where men are referred to using the category "man", they most often appear as "the man", the definite article making them sound like a piece of a puzzle rather than active participants in the process of creating children. This is compounded by the fact that "man" or "the man" only ever appears in co-text with "sperm donor" or "donor" in this article, whether in the same or adjacent sentences. In this discourse of fatherless conception, men are configured as the passive suppliers of a commodity or reduced to the commodity itself.

Discussion

The lesbian identity constructed in *Diva* draws heavily on notions of "us" and "them" – frequently "us" *versus* "them". In this construction are moves from what van Dijk calls the "ideological square", in which writers emphasise the positives and suppress the negatives about "us", while expressing the negatives and de-emphasising the positives about "them" (1998, 267). In *Diva's* case, this is often a very defensive operation, configuring "them" as a constant source of attack or the threat of attack. They are institutionally set against "us", deny "us" the safety and privilege "they" grant "themselves" and are prepared to make great personal sacrifice in pursuit of maintaining this *status quo*. By contrast, "we", for all our disadvantage, enjoy something liberating and extraordinary that remains beyond "their" grasp.

This is understandable given the situational and social contexts of the time. The writers and editors of *Diva*, as the producers of a (unique and) distinctly lesbian magazine are addressing a reader looking for news from "our" viewpoint, a connection with remote (in-group) others and, crucially, positive self-identification. It is perhaps an unfortunate necessity to take any opportunities available to affirm in-group identity even at the cost of cultivating hostilities with other groups. The reader comes to the magazine in what was, as discussed above, a crucial period for gay politics. In several areas of social life, equality was on the horizon, but this had brought vocal opposition from certain quarters and with it a feeling of exposure; and equality had been on the horizon for some time without coming into view. The Labour Party's manifesto promises of 1997 regarding Section 28, for instance, had stalled on more than one occasion, which is perhaps why we find this recognisable discourse of distrust.

The same scepticism and sense of threat is evident in what we might call a "queer ideological square", in which bisexuals and gay men become "them". They are a threat for making permeable the boundaries between "us" and "them", or by being domineering but necessary political allies. Although *Diva* pays lip-service to the more inclusive "queer girl" discourse in its strapline shift – making a highly visible statement to potential readers – the "self" is drawn very markedly as lesbian. As Extract 3 shows, a picture of bisexuals as stealthy, promiscuous opportunists (Humphrey 1999) is more likely to be propounded than quashed. *Diva's* treatment of gay men speaks to a reader aware of the convenience of remaining allied as "lesbians and gay men" in the public battle for tolerance and equality, but one who wishes to make clear the cultural differences between them.

This handling of the in-group and external others is symptomatic of a group accustomed to seeing itself as "other" in everyday discourse, the constant feelings of exclusion fostering a reliance on the building of boundaries and a discourse enabling them to deride those parts of hegemonic culture towards which they feel antipathy or to which they are denied access (Eves 2004; Rodgers 1972). A (critical) discourse analysis has shown how the relationship between "us" and a heterosexual "them" continues to be manufactured in terms of a combative binary in which "we" are the victims of "their" heteropatriarchal oppression, and how those discriminatory dynamics (Humphrey 1999, 224) can be reproduced in a queer context in the pursuit of positive, apparently authentic self-identification.

Notes

1. As stated online, June 2007: http://www.divamag.co.uk.
2. By publishers Millivres Prowler.

3. In personal correspondence.
4. Clause in Britain's Local Government Act 1988, which prevented local authorities from "promoting homosexuality".
5. P. Hitchens, Cowards made police carry guns and the can, *Mail on Sunday*, 22 July 2001. Available from http://www.mailonsunday.co.uk/debate/columnists/article-117627/Cowards-police -carry-guns-can.html.
6. J. Travis, Milking the revolution, *Diva*, October 2002, p. 28.
7. K. Wildblood, No airs and a lot of grace, *Diva*, September 2002, p. 55.
8. E. Gill, The return of Anna Nolan, *Diva*, August 2002, p. 40.
9. T. Wilton, Hidden treasures, *Diva*, August 2002, pp. 33–34.
10. L. Saffron, Donor insemination at a clinic – with a known donor, *Diva*, August 2002, p. 51.
11. R.V. Woodgate, Aussie girls rule!, *Diva*, October 2002, pp. 38–41.
12. Equal rights opponent dies, *Diva*, November 2002, p. 23.
13. See note 10.
14. G. Rodgerson, From the editor, *Diva*, August 2002, p. 4; *emphasis* in original, underline my addition.
15. S. Katz, Slow dance and stickers: Boston dyke march, *Diva*, August 2002, p. 20.
16. K. Wildblood, Beat of the sun, *Diva*, December 2002, pp. 62–63.
17. See note 9.
18. A. Glenny, Frida's other loves, *Diva*, August 2002, pp. 36–37.
19. E. Brown, Maybe I do, maybe I don't, *Diva*, September 2002, pp. 19–20.
20. C. Cooper, Sperm wars, *Diva*, September 2002, pp. 36–37.
21. M. Gray, The rights of our children, *Diva*, September 2002, pp. 38–39.

References

Ballaster, R., M. Beetham, E. Frazer, and S. Hebron. 1991. *Women's worlds: Ideology, femininity and the woman's magazine.* London: Macmillan.

Benwell, B. 2003. *Masculinity and men's lifestyle magazines.* Oxford: Blackwell.

Berelson, B. 1971. *Content analysis in communication research.* New York: Hafner.

Boni, F. 2002. Framing media masculinities: Men's lifestyle magazines and the biopolitics of the male body. *European Journal of Communication* 17: 465–78.

Crewe, B. 2003. *Representing men: Cultural production and producers in the men's magazine market.* Oxford: Berg.

Driver, S. 2007. *Queer girls and popular culture: Reading, resisting and creating media.* Oxford: Peter Lang.

Eggins, S., and R. Iedema. 1997. Difference without diversity: Semantic orientation and ideology in competing women's magazines. In *Gender and discourse*, ed. R. Wodak, 165–96. London: Sage.

Eves, A. 2004. Queer theory, butch/femme identities and lesbian space. *Sexualities* 7 4: 480–96.

Fairclough, N. 1989. *Language and power.* London: Longman.

———. 1995. *Critical discourse analysis.* London: Longman.

Fairclough, N. , and R. Wodak . 1997. Critical discourse analysis: An overview. In *Discourse Studies: A multidisciplinary introduction*, ed. T. van Dijk, Vol. 2, 67–97. London: Sage.

Ferguson, M. 1983. *Forever feminine: Women's magazines and the cult of femininity.* London: Heinemann.

Humphrey, J.C. 1999. To queer or not to queer a lesbian and gay group? Sexual and gendered politics at the turn of the century. *Sexualities* 2, no. 2: 223–46.

Kim, J.L., and L.M. Ward. 2004. Pleasure reading: associations between young women's sexual attitudes and their reading of contemporary women's magazines. *Psychology of Women Quarterly* 28, no. 1: 48–58.

Livia, A. 2002. *Camionneuses s'abstenir*: Lesbian community creation through the personals. In *Language and sexuality: Contesting meaning in theory and practice*, ed. K. Campbell-Kibler et al., 190–207. Stanford: California Center for the Study of Language and Information.

Martin, B. 1996. *Femininity played straight: The significance of being lesbian.* London: Routledge.

McCracken, E. 1993. *Decoding women's magazines: From Mademoiselle to Ms.* Basingstoke: Macmillan.

McLoughlin, L. 2000. *The language of magazines.* London: Routledge.

Miller, C., and K. Swift. 1976. *Words and women: New language in new times.* London: Victor Gollancz.

Peterson, T. 1964. *Magazines in the twentieth century.* Urbana: University of Illinois Press.

Phillips, L., and M. Jørgensen. 2002. *Discourse analysis as theory and method.* London: Sage.

Richardson, J.E. 2006. *Analysing newspapers: An approach from critical discourse analysis.* Basingstoke: Palgrave Macmillan.

Rodgers, B. 1972. *The Queen's vernacular: A gay lexicon.* London: Blond Briggs.

van Dijk, T. 1998. *Ideology.* London: Sage.

Wilton, T. 1995. *Lesbian studies: Setting an agenda.* London: Routledge.

Winston, B. 1990. On counting the wrong things. In *The media reader,* ed. M. Alvarado and J.B. Thompson, 50–64. London: BFI.

Wong, A., and Q. Zhang. 2001. The linguistic construction of the Tóngzhì community. *Journal of Linguistic Anthropology* 10, no. 2: 248–78.

Wood, L., and R. Kroger. 2000. *Doing discourse analysis: Methods for studying action in talk and text.* London: Sage.

The dilemma of frugality and consumption in British women's magazines 1940–1955

Joseph D. Burridge

The present paper is based upon a corpus of texts drawn from women's magazines published whilst a policy of rationing was in effect in Britain. It problematises the way in which some debates about the significance of frugality and consumption at that time have been constructed – in an either/or manner. As an alternative, it advocates a more dilemmatic, and messier, approach that can better grasp the nuanced ways in which frugality was also used as a resource to incite consumption of specific items. The paper maps some of the ways in which food adverts positioned the product depicted in relation to rationing and war, and explores their rhetorical construction in more detail, demonstrating the ways in which categorising adverts as frugality-orientated or consumption-orientated is insufficient to understand the claims offered about the product. Attention is also directed towards adverts for products explicitly identified as unavailable, and in particular the approach adopted by Stork Margarine in this regard – substituting their product with a "cookery service" to assist the "housewife" with the difficulties of rationing.

Introduction

The present paper examines a corpus of advertisements drawn from women's magazines published during and after the Second World War while a policy of rationing was in place in Britain. It provides an empirically-based account of the rhetorical strategies that were used to position goods in relation to the war and the rationing policy between 1940 – the year that rationing began – and 1955 – the year *after* it ended. The paper addresses two competing narratives concerned with this period of history – one emphasising an ideology of frugality, and an alternative that identifies a drive towards consumption – exemplified by the competing accounts of Witkowski (2003) and Adkins Covert (2003).

I aim to problematise these opposing trajectories, by exploring some of the ways that adverts for food orientate towards the scarcity of items *at the same time* as advocating their consumption. I do so by drawing on the concept of the "ideological dilemma" from Billig et al. (1988), who demonstrate the value of treating ideology as fundamentally *two-sided*. On this understanding, rather than producing singular programmes for action, ideology produces "dilemmatic quandaries" that have to be actively resolved in everyday life (Billig et al. 1988, 146). Extrapolating a little, it becomes important to explore how contrary pressures play off one another, and how the apparent tensions between them are resolved in practice by those affected by them.

Amouzadeh and Tavangar (2004) take some of these issues seriously in work on advertisements from post-revolutionary Iran, and specifically on their use of pictorial metaphors to reconcile two competing ideologies – the commercial imperative of advertising and the so-called "Islamic values" distilled in Iran's ban on the portrayal of women in advertisements. Exploring adverts for beauty products, they focus on how the strategies used to balance these competing ideologies compensate for the lack of images of women by metaphorically substituting flowers, pearls, nature, clothing and the moon (Amouzadeh and Tavanger 2004, 161, 171). They show, therefore, how apparently opposing imperatives do not simply restrict options, but also afford creative opportunities for reconciling such opposition (Amouzadeh and Tavangar 2004, 147–148) – in this case between commercialism and "Islamic values".

It is with this in mind that I turn to some relevant literature concerned with rationing, and the extent to which it tends to offer us competing, but largely one-sided, accounts of the significance of food advertising during and immediately after the war.

Literature and historical context

After much preparation, a policy of war-time rationing was launched in Britain in 1940, and lasted until 1954. Various goods were placed under a system of centralised administrative control, in order for sufficient supplies to be maintained. People's access to foods such as meat, tea, fats and oils, flour, cheese, and eggs were all directly affected by the policy, with the amounts available fluctuating considerably throughout the war. Once the war was over, rationing of most goods continued. The rationing of flour eventually ended in 1948, and other items were de-rationed in the years that followed (canned and dried fruit in 1950, tea in 1952, and sugar in 1953), until all food rationing ended in July 1954.

Detailed social scientific studies of the British rationing policy are rare, and those taking seriously magazines and advertisements even rarer. Those in existence vary in the degree to which they focus upon specific texts, or tell a very general story for other purposes. The most comprehensive account of the history of rationing policy in Britain is Zweiniger-Bargielowska's (2000) book-length treatment, charting its origins, administration, operation and reception. The closest equivalent for the United States would be Bentley's (1998) account, which offers a more sociologically-orientated story about the enhanced national importance of housewifery and motherhood. Zweiniger-Bargielowska (2000, 110), in particular, notes how the "food propaganda" in magazines consisted largely of advice about economy, nutrition, and variety in the face of shortages.

Several accounts of the contemporary and historical significance of women's magazines also cover the impact of war, often claiming that magazines became "disseminators of information and morale-boosters" (Ballaster et al. 1991, 110) while foregrounding the nation's needs over those of the individual and family (Winship 1987, 31). White (1970) discusses magazines' emphasis upon ingenuity and the practicalities of coping with scarcity during the war, and claims that the space available for adverts was reduced substantially, resulting in "short messages underlining the persistence of war-time scarcity and war-time priorities" (White 1970, 124). In their detailed account of the content of British woman's magazines during the war, Waller and Vaughan-Rees (1987) note the strong presence of advice for "making do" – including regular Ministry of Food "Bulletins", and the more general portrayal of food as a "munition of war" (Waller and Vaughan-Rees 1987, 49; also see Witkowski 2003, 73–74). Interestingly, they claim that a very prevalent advertising theme was that "there seemed to be no product, from underwear to cigarettes, from sewing machines to biscuits which was not needed '*more than ever*' before" (Waller and Vaughan-Rees 1987, 94; original emphasis). The implication is that the occurrence of war was actually used to sell products – it altered and intensified certain advertising strategies.

These various accounts leave us with a limited picture regarding the significance of frugality and consumption, and detailed studies of more direct topical relevance tend to be geographically focused upon the United States, where, following the United States' entry into the war, a comparable system of rationing, which controlled availability of a similar range of food items – sugar, fats, meat, canned goods – was put in place by the Office of Price Administration (Bentley 1998, 15–24), until the war ended.

A very important contribution to the narrative of frugality and restraint comes from Witkowski (2003, 69), who focuses on the US Government's "ideology of frugal consumption". He focuses upon government poster campaigns, and identifies five main practices that were praised regularly within their content – conservation, recycling, home food production, rationing, and saving through the American war bond scheme – and notes the way in which the abundant advice was targeted at women who were assigned responsibility for their implementation (Witkowski 2003, 77–78).

More importantly, for present purposes, Witkowski implies that frugality and consumption are *not* mutually exclusive options since much commercial advertising during the war included frugality themes and direct appeals to consume less (Witkowski 2003, 79). It is important, therefore, not to assume a clear and neat picture of the significance of frugality and consumption where a more messy understanding would be far more appropriate. Nevertheless, Witkowski's emphasis is firmly upon the significance of frugality and its allegedly generalised construction as a nationally desirable imperative at the time.

In a significant critique of this view, Adkins Covert (2003) explored the idea that American women were significantly confronted with "messages" advocating *unrestricted consumption* rather than frugality. Based on a quantitative content analysis of American magazine *Ladies Home Journal*, she concluded that, during the war, American women were confronted with a "consistent message of unrestricted consumption" (Adkins Covert 2003, 315). She claims that consumers were asked to "direct their desire to consume unavailable products into purchasing products that were available in ample supply" (Adkins Covert 2003, 328). This oversimplifies matters to the extent that it does not allow for the possibility that *an advert can do more than one thing at a time*, and the rhetorical complexity of each advert is lost in pursuit of the ability to make claims about prevalence at a particular time period, and diachronic change across it. To be fair, Adkins Covert (2003, 317–318) does discuss the "contradictions" between dominant messages of frugality and consumption. Nevertheless, rather than confronting this as a rhetorical problem for the advertisers, she tends to focus upon the extent to which it was functional for the national interest – a commercially lucrative process of self-justification and an adjustment to the needs of the economy in wartime.

While it is recognised in some of these accounts that frugality and consumption are not simply mutually exclusive, what is missing is the extent to which the rationing policy was both a rhetorical problem *and* an opportunity – this two-sidedness is heavily understated. The only account that comes close in this regard is Parkin's (2006) discussion of the content of American adverts published during the Second World War. She identifies the interrelation between frugality and consumption by noting that war offered the opportunity for companies to encourage consumption of their brand by claiming that their product was healthy, economical and patriotic, *at the same time* as encouraging frugality (Parkin 2006, 94–95). As well as being a problem, rationing was also a *resource* for advertisers – it was something that could be invoked and used in various ways.

It is important to clarify that this article will not adjudicate this debate. Instead, I am suggesting that the framing of the debate about frugality *or* consumption is misplaced since advertisers, themselves, formulate multiple ways of handling the tension between the two imperatives, and even use it as a resource. This means that I am viewing the adverts as primarily the *outcome* of a process – addressing problems for the producers and advertisers – rather than as the beginning of a process of influence. I am not operating in the realm of "effects", and accept that magazines are better indices of the concerns of editors, authors and advertisers, than the experience of their readers (Zweiniger-Bargielowska 2000, 101–102; Parkin 2006, 5).

Methodological reflections

The materials upon which this paper is based are drawn from a corpus of data generated for the Leverhulme-funded "Changing Families, Changing Food" Programme at the University of Sheffield. The corpus consists of 2544 magazines articles concerned with food and its provision, drawn from 144 issues of the magazines *Woman's Own* (*WO*) and *Woman and Home* (*WH*) published between 1940 and 2006.

Here, attention is focused upon those magazines that were published between 1940, when rationing began, and 1955, the year *after* food control ended in Britain. This temporal focus includes 37 of the magazines, and yields a subgroup of 569 articles, editorials, recipes and adverts. Of these texts, 456 (80.1%) items are explicitly commercial advertisements, and of these 65 (14.3%) render thematic some aspect of rationing or war. Discounting adverts that are exactly the same but appear more than once leaves 62, and it is upon these items that I concentrate – giving a general sense of the positioning strategies used to construct the significance of the war, and then analysing a few instances in greater detail to show the value of problematising the more singular accounts already discussed. These materials were treated as rhetorical constructions – discursive entities with detectable persuasive trajectories – and were confronted with the following question: how do they position the product in relation to rationing or war, and frugality and/or consumption?

The following analysis includes some discussion of issues such as layout and font where relevant; however, my emphasis is primarily upon the way the linguistic elements of the advertisements rhetorically position the product depicted in relation to frugality and/or consumption. Compared with contemporary magazine advertisements, the corpus tends to consist of relatively long copy – adverts with extensive portions of text relative to their pictorial content (Cook 2001, 16) – so while not exactly desirable, this limiting of focus can be forgiven.

Mapping the rhetorical strategies

It is useful to offer an initial summary of the ways in which the relevant material in the corpus is positioned in relation to rationing and war, before going on to discuss some interesting examples in greater detail. In the interests of providing an overview of the 84 instances of such positioning (several adverts contained more than one such strategy) I grouped the adverts into seven broad categories. Table 1 presents the number of the adverts in the corpus that contained each of these seven strategies.

Table 1. Incidence of positioning strategies, by magazine (1940–1955).

	Woman's Own	Woman & Home	Total
Product is available and a solution or substitute for rationed goods	35	6	41
Product is available, because it is "essential"	2	1	3
Product is the same as pre-war, or, better now	4	0	4
Product is scarce – but worth it when you get it	7	0	7
Product is currently unavailable – provision of a substitute service	3	3	6
Product is currently unavailable – it will be back soon	8	3	11
The product is back now or available again	9	3	12
Total	68	16	84

The first four categories include: adverts claiming that the product was currently available and offered as a substitute or solution; those claiming that the product was essential; was no different in quality; or was available but scarce . The next two categories map claims that the product was unavailable, distinguished by the offering of a service as substitute, and claims that the product would be "back soon". The final category includes those instances claiming that, having been unavailable previously, the product is back again.

As we can see, the most recurrent strategy evident in the corpus in both magazines, particularly in *WO*, is that the product is a solution to the problems of rationing or a substitute for rationed goods – it directly addresses frugality in some way. The low amount of material drawn from *WH*, however, makes meaningful comparison between the magazines difficult, and they are therefore better treated in aggregate rather than being differentiated. The amount of variation between the prevalence of other strategies is not large, but, as I discuss below, the "substitute service" category is particularly interesting.

In the following two sections, I blend together the general characterisation of evident regularities in the content, quoting relevant portions of some adverts and giving more detailed consideration of some specific instances – an advert for Ovaltine, and a campaign for Stork Margarine's "Cookery Service". These are followed by a discussion that restates the case for a dilemmatic understanding of the relationship between frugality and consumption.

Available products: substitutions, solutions and essentials

Adverts for some products proudly proclaimed their status as unaffected by rationing. Adverts for Cadbury's Bournville Cocoa and Rowntree's Hot Chocolate (*WO* 2 June 1944, 16, 23) during this period tended to end with the legend "Cocoa is Still Unrationed" – attempting to make a virtue out of their availability despite the restrictions in place elsewhere.

Adverts for other products, not content with merely being available, were claimed to be available in the face of hardship. Scott's Emulsion of Cod Liver Oil (*WO* 3 December 1943, 12) claimed that "the value of cod liver oil has been recognized by the Government, who have made supplies available" because of its "important part in rebuilding the health of British children" after World War One. An advert for Ribena (*WH* June 1960, 65) also claimed the intervention of the government, asserting that the product was only available in sufficient supply "[t]hanks to Ministry of Food help". The upshot in both these cases is that the products are so essential that the government was moved to intervene to ensure their continued supply – amounting to a claim of government endorsement.

A warrant offered recurrently by adverts is that the product is a solution to a problem (Cook 2001, 49; Dyer 1982, 168–169), and this is often a problem that is constructed by the same advert. Williamson (1978, 146) discusses the way in which Lea & Perrins sauce has often been advertised as offering the opportunity for the *improvement* of food via a process akin to a magical transformation. This has been a recurrent theme throughout the history of such flavouring products, but was linked directly to the war and the rationing of meat in the corpus. Such ingredients were claimed to compensate for the absence of other foods by transforming the taste, and stretching the quantities, of those that were available:

> Catering for a family was never easy even in normal times. Now with certain foods rationed, supplies of others limited and prices rising, it is really difficult. But whatever food we serve we can make the most of and the *best* of it with proper seasoning. (Lea & Perrins, *WO* 13 July 1940, 25; original emphasis)

The existence of rationing was used similarly by other similar products such as Bovril (*WO* 2 June 1944, 23) and Bisto (*WO* 13 October 1949, 32). These adverts all use rationing as a resource to *intensify* a reason usually given for purchasing such products – that they *transform* what they are used with – but this is given extra weight in the context of rationing, with the purchase and use of the specific product portrayed as a solution to the problems associated with a more generalised frugality.

I now turn to a more considered examination of an advert for Ovaltine. This brings together some of these themes with a more complex usage of the relevance of frugality and consumption than fits with accounts that emphasise the significance of one or the other.

The advert for Ovaltine (Figure 1) features a large picture of one of the brand's recurring motifs – a dairymaid – carrying some barley, a basket of eggs and holding forth a tin of Ovaltine in the direction of the audience. The outward and downward direction of this gesture, combined with the goods she is holding, seems to imply generosity: that the viewer is offered the product as a gift because she has plenty. Inset are two smaller and less detailed circular bordered pictures on either side of the central character's lower body that depict locations for consumption of the product.

Importantly, given the large emboldened text that follows immediately below the picture, and above the more extended textual sections – "How Ovaltine helps you and the Country too" – the central character is wearing a sash labelled "on national service".

From only these two elements we can see a dual purpose being constructed for the product: it is of help to you *and* the country, and this is reinforced by the labelled sash. To purchase and use it is neither a fundamentally selfish act, nor an act of self-denial in the national interest. There is a denial of a dilemma here – by buying and using Ovaltine you can have it both ways – have your drink and drink it.

Beneath the composite picture, on the right-hand side of the advert there is a section headed by the claim "Ovaltine provides ALL the Essential Food Properties", which consists of three short bullet-points, each elaborated by a paragraph of text. Apart from the initial "Ovaltine", all of this is italicised – which, along with the bullet-point structure, marks it out as separate from the extended text on the left.

Although not mentioned directly, these three "points" address more or less exactly the British Ministry of Food's preferred typology of food groups that was circulated at the time as a simplified educational tool. These three groups – building, energising and protecting foods (simpler than even the US "Basic Seven" food groups; see Bentley 1998,

Woman's Own, July 13, 1940

How Ovaltine helps you and the Country too

TO exercise food economy . . . to get the best out of available foods and, consequently, to relieve pressure on our shipping . . . are the vitally important measures in which the country asks for your co-operation.

There are definite reasons why the regular use of delicious 'Ovaltine' will help you in this national duty. 'Ovaltine' is a product of Britain's farms and fields, and possesses all the nutritive elements needed to make your dietary really complete.

Prepared from Nature's finest protective and restorative foods, 'Ovaltine' provides in a concentrated and correctly balanced form the carbohydrates, proteins, mineral salts and other nutritive elements essential to good health and vitality. Its vitamin content is also outstanding.

Moreover, 'Ovaltine' possesses exceptional nerve-restoring properties—so much needed in these nerve-wearing days—which are largely derived from the new-laid eggs liberally used in its manufacture. *No tonic food beverage could be complete without eggs.*

Furthermore, 'Ovaltine' is exceptionally economical in use. The small size tin will make as many as 24 cupfuls of delicious, health-giving nourishment.

For all these reasons, make 'Ovaltine' the regular daily beverage for every member of your family. The more you use 'Ovaltine' the less you will feel the curtailment of rationed foods. Moreover, 'Ovaltine' will make a definite improvement in the nutritive value of the family dietary.

Ovaltine

provides ALL the Essential Food Properties

● *Nutriment for Body, Brain & Nerves*

'Ovaltine' provides in scientifically correct proportions and in easily digestible form the nutritive elements required for building up perfect fitness of body, brain and nerves.

● *Energy–giving Properties*

'Ovaltine' provides in abundance the carbohydrates, proteins and other nutritive elements that create ample reserves of energy and vitality.

● *Protective Food Elements*

'Ovaltine' provides the important vitamins A, B1, B2 and D and other protective food properties so necessary for maintaining robust health and physical fitness.

Drink
Ovaltine
HOT or COLD
For Health, Strength and all-day Energy

Figure 1.   Ovaltine advert (*WO* 13 July 1940, 5).

68–70) – appear explicitly elsewhere in the corpus, and anyone reading the magazines at the time would have had difficulty avoiding them.

In this portion of the advert, each element in the typology is addressed by one of the bullet-points (although "building" is only mentioned in the paragraph beneath the heading). By arguing that Ovaltine provides each of these properties – it builds, it energises, and it protects – and explaining how it does so, the advert is able to demonstrate its "completeness". By providing each, it does *everything* officially required of food at the time, as well as being economical and efficient. This also means that the advert serves as an example of the synthesis of health, economy, and patriotism identified by Parkin (2006, 94–95).

In the extended text below the picture on the left-hand side of the advert, three things are set up as requirements that the audience is being asked to fulfil at present – three measures with which "you" have to co-operate. In the next paragraph, these are retroactively fused in elliptical fashion (the three measures becoming "this national duty"), and Ovaltine is offered as a solution to the implicit "problem" that this duty poses. The product is claimed to be home-grown, and therefore puts no pressure on shipping, and contributes to food economy and efficient nutrition by possessing "all the nutritive elements needed to make your dietary really complete".

Most important, for present purposes, are the final two paragraphs. The first of these connects with regularly-made claims during this period about the relationship between beverages and "nerves" – the drink's "nerve-restoring properties" – and linking this to the "new-laid eggs" it contains. The following sentence claims that "No tonic food beverage could be complete without eggs", something that constructs a criterion for "completeness", and emphasises that Ovaltine meets that criterion. As well as a positive presentation of the product, this is arguably also a distinction device in relation to the competition – the type of practice anticipated by Williamson (1978, 24–5; Cook 2001, 68) – constructing an unnamed, and inferior, competing product (which contains no eggs and is therefore *incomplete*) as less worthy of purchase.

The final paragraph restates the extent of Ovaltine's economical powers, quantifies the number of cups obtainable from a single small tin, and reaches a conclusion, restating that the preceding points constitute a reason for buying and using Ovaltine. Then we arrive at the *key* point in relation to rationing and the frugality/consumption dilemma: "The more you use 'Ovaltine' the less you will feel the curtailment of rationed goods". Again, here we have the familiar problem–solution logic (Cook 2001; Dyer 1982) on show, but the sentence also orientates to both "sides" of the frugality/consumption dilemma. According to the advert, the scarcity of rationed goods is a problem and has a commercial solution – the purchase and regular use of Ovaltine – which will help you to not notice the reduced availability of those other goods.

Ovaltine, therefore, is something that reduces the impact of rationing upon you (and your family), and helps you to co-operate with the prevalent national requirements for efficiency that are at stake. This is far too subtle to be satisfactorily categorised as either consumption-orientated or frugality-orientated. Instead, the advert shows how, even in an instance advocating consumption, frugality can be central as a resource, since the incitement to consume is particularised, and places frugality centre-stage – if you buy *this* product you will not notice the absence of others. Buying it therefore constitutes a substitute for more widespread consumption, which will be unnecessary since Ovaltine will help you deal with that more generalised absence. Accordingly, the encouragement of consumption does not automatically negate an ideology of frugality since if you consume the correct products then this can itself be frugal! This makes a clear separation between frugality and consumption, or the use of some zero-sum logic, insufficiently complex to make sense of how they are *used* within advertisements. What we need, instead, is a more nuanced account that explores the resolution of any purported tension between them.

Unavailable products: reminders and substitute services

While the corpus contains some advertisements featuring apologies for a product's *limited* availability, there are also several adverts that admit to a product being *unavailable*. A few of these approximate apologies for the product's imminent disappearance, and several of these adverts also offer predictions for the product's future availability – a vaunted return "with victory" in the war (Robertson's Golden Shred Marmalade [*WO* 2 June 1944, 3], Turban Mixed Fruit [*WO* 7 December 1945]). These adverts bolster the account of unavailability via attaching it to patriotic purposes – an orientation towards the importance of the war as something significant beyond the personal inconvenience of going without specific foods.

The most recurrent adverts for unavailable products, in this corpus, came from Stork Margarine, and all six of the adverts that fall into the "substitute service" category are for the brand. With this in mind I turn to a more detailed consideration of four of these adverts.[1]

In order to understand these adverts, it is helpful to know that margarine was rationed in Britain from July 1940 until July 1954 (Zweiniger-Bargielowska 2000, 18). The margarine industry engaged in a collective and voluntary de-branding in 1940, a decision that it framed in expectable patriotic terms, and came under the control of a single organisation called Marcome Ltd, which was connected to the wartime Ministry of Food (Margarine and Spread Association 2007; Stork Margarine Cookery Service 1995, iii). The de-branding of margarine meant that the brand – Stork, along with its rivals – underwent a literal loss of its distinctiveness since, although the product was still manufactured, it was not labelled as such where purchased. For these purposes, the margarine industry was also legally required to "vitaminise" its product so as to reduce the differences between it and butter, with which it was categorised for rationing purposes.

While some food products, such as gravies and flavourings were portrayed as substitutions for ingredients that were unavailable or whose availability was limited, Stork actually created *a substitute for its own product* – a free "Cookery Service", which still exists today in a modified form – which responded to food-related questions posed by housewives in response to their "rationing difficulties". This substitution is not quite a metaphorical substitution of the form understood by Amouzadeh and Tavanger (2004), but it is similar. Since the margarine itself was not available, a substitute service was put in place with the same brand name attached to it, to keep the name in circulation, even when the branded margarine was not.

The temporally-bounded corpus contains seven adverts for Stork Margarine's "Cookery Service", six of which were published while the margarine itself was unavailable due to the de-branding (see Figure 2).[2] Rather than analysing each advert individually, I am most interested in the regularities across these four, and there are five main dimensions, with minor variations, which merit attention.

First of all, all four adverts feature an emboldened and capitalised "STORK MARGARINE COOKERY SERVICE" in the same typeface. In the first three chronologically, this is a heading; and in the fourth, this same text is positioned at the foot of the advert instead. In all five adverts this is the largest text visible, and in all cases "STORK MARGARINE" is on top of "COOKERY SERVICE". This arguably makes

STORK MARGARINE COOKERY SERVICE

NEW flavours — that's the way to keep your meals *alive*. And that's where the Stork Cookery Service can help you with its free advice. One day Stork Margarine will be back — meanwhile you'll be delighted with these monthly leaflets describing dishes that are both tasty and economical.

CURRIES

Curry will often add interest to your meal-table, and with the colder weather coming on these dishes are ideal. Stork Leaflet No. 122 gives you many recipes for delicious dishes which can be flavoured with curry.

COUPON — CUT THIS OUT NOW

Send this coupon in an unsealed 1d-stamped envelope to The Stork Margarine Cookery Service, Dept. 183, Unilever House, London, E.C.4 for Cookery Notes No. 122 "Curries".

Name ....

Street ....

Town ....

JSC 231-84

(*WO* 12 October 1950, 26).

STORK MARGARINE COOKERY SERVICE

CHRISTMAS finds us ready once again with more helpful recipes and ideas for the housewife. Many housewives use the Stork Margarine Cookery Service all the year round, while they are waiting for Stork to return. The Service is free and so practical too!

CHRISTMAS COOKERY

Just now you'll want those extra-special recipes that make Christmas meals such a delight. Stork Leaflet No. 123 has a selection of recipes for Christmas Cakes, Puddings and Pies that will make the family wish it were Christmas every day.

COUPON — CUT THIS OUT NOW

Send this coupon in an unsealed 1d-stamped envelope to the Stork Margarine Cookery Service, Dept. 193, Unilever House, London, E.C.4, for Cookery Notes No. 123 "Christmas Cookery".

Name ....

Street ....

Town ....

JSC 254-96

(*WH* December 1950, 59)

STORK MARGARINE COOKERY SERVICE

A 20-page booklet telling you...

"ALL ABOUT PASTRY"

Here is yet another free booklet from the Stork Cookery Service, accompanied by a leaflet of handy, everyday recipes. You'll find out how to make different types of pastry, how to be sure of success, and how to avoid failures.

Stork Margarine is not yet back in the shops, but we are always ready to help you with advice. If you have any cooking problem at all, send it along to us and we'll solve it for you.

CUT THIS OUT NOW

COUPON

Send this coupon in an unsealed 1½d-stamped envelope to The Stork Margarine Cookery Service, Dept. H193, Unilever House, London, E.C.4 for your copy of "All About Pastry" and Leaflet No. 132 "Pastry Recipes — Sweet, Meat and Savoury".

Name ....

Street ....

Town ....

JSC 329-99

(*WH* November 1952, 19)

Cooking Problems Vanish!

Never live with a cooking snag! Send it to the Stork Margarine Cookery Service, and let us make it disappear for you! Don't forget that Stork Margarine itself will be back in the shops shortly. Meanwhile we're always here ready to send you advice and answer your cooking queries.

STORK MARGARINE COOKERY SERVICE

DEPT. 193, 9 GREAT SUFFOLK STREET, LONDON, S.E.1

JSC 377-96

(*WH* January 1954, 68)

Figure 2. Adverts for Stork Margarine's "Cookery Service".

clear that it is the Stork Margarine-ness that is central. That is, although it is the same size as "Cookery Service", it is positioned above – which, in such compositions, tends to imply its greater significance (see Machin 2007).

Secondly, all four adverts feature the product's trademark "Stork" figure. In the earliest two, the Stork is in its conventional side-on pose, standing on one of its legs. In the latter two the trademark has become an anthropomorphised character, depicted with its "mouth" wide open. In the first of these, the Stork is sat down on a seat reading an "All about pastry" book, which is part of what is advertised in the rest of the piece (*WH* November 1952, 19), while the last one shows him/her posed with a top hat and a "magic wand" pointed at a heading "Cooking problems vanish!" – amounting to the claim that the Stork Margarine Cookery Service performs such a magical feat.

Thirdly, each of the four adverts stresses that the service is a practical and effective solution to rationing difficulties. They all orientate towards the problems of rationing – the assumption is that balancing issues of taste and economy and day-to-day food provision is a problem, especially on festive occasions such as Christmas (*WH* December 1950, 59). Imposed frugality is therefore a problem with which women are currently faced. The first three of the four feature coupons that can be cut out and sent off in exchange for monthly numbered "Cooking Notes" prepared by Unilever/Stork for "housewives", which advise on how to manage with the restrictions imposed by rationing. It is not a huge leap to suggest that the service was meeting a need, given the wider prevalence of requests for advice in women's magazines at the time (White 1970, 132).

Fourthly, all four adverts also refer to the service as being free or available in an unrestricted way, implying that provision of the service is generous – perhaps a gift – as well as being both helpful and practical. Now, the "gift" of a recipe was a relatively frequent feature of food advertisements at the time, so we should not overstate how innovative this was. However, the fact that the product itself was unavailable distinguishes Stork in this regard. Trying to make sense of the intended pay-off from providing this service is necessarily speculative, but it seems reasonable to think that the generosity and helpful nature of the service is supposed to form an intimate connection – the construction of a personal relationship between the "housewife" and Stork margarine – storing up good sentiments for the future when the actual product returns and Unilever can commercially benefit more clearly from it being consumed. That, of course, does not undermine any utility that the service may have had for individuals making use of it.

The final central element common to all four adverts reinforces this conclusion about the pay-off via a statement about Stork's current absence but *eventual return* – emphasising that the free service is an interim, stop-gap affair – a temporary substitute for the product. The temporary nature is made clear in the following ways: "One day Stork Margarine will be back …" (*WO* 12 October 1950, 26), " … while they are waiting for Stork to return" (*WH* December 1950, 59), " … not yet back in the shops, but …" (*WH* November 1952, 19), and "Stork Margarine itself will be back in the shops shortly. Meanwhile …" (*WH* January 1954, 68). The last of these four excerpts, in particular, with its use of "itself", emphasises that the "Cookery Service" is not "really" what is advertised. This fits with the claim that it is "STORK MARGARINE" and not the "COOKERY SERVICE" that is of ultimate importance, and supports the conclusion that circulation of the brand name is the ultimate priority here (see White 1970, 124).

As with the Ovaltine advertisement, it is unclear how this campaign would fit in relation to a narrative stressing frugality *or* consumption. The adverts are to some degree about coping with the imposed frugality, but also seem designed to encourage consumption of the particular product once it returns, and via the brand having helped with the problems of frugality.

Discussion

Despite the restricted nature of the corpus on which this paper is based, I have raised several issues that deserve to be addressed more systematically in future work on the representation of food and the significance of advertising during the historical period in which British rationing was in place.

In their advocacy of the concept of the ideological dilemma, Billig et al. (1988, 4) position themselves against both theories of cognition and theories of ideology by claiming to have found in their empirical material more ideological influence than the cognitive theorists would predict, and more evidence of dilemmatic thought than theorists of ideology would expect – things were more complex than either set of theories would tend to accommodate. When it comes to the relationship between frugality and consumption during Second World War rationing, things are similarly more complex than previous accounts would expect, even allowing for my interest in a different nation-state. While both Witkowski (2003), with his emphasis on the ideology of frugality, and Adkins Covert (2003), with her emphasis on unrestricted consumption, do acknowledge the alternative imperative in their respective but opposing accounts, I think that it is fair to say that this material shows evidence of a more messy and complex relationship between frugality and consumption than either might expect. In particular, I have shown some of the ways in which the two can combine in subtle ways that make generalisations about the primary influence of one or the other insufficiently rich to understand the nuances of relationship between them when it comes to advertisements for food in Britain while rationing was in place.

I am not arguing that what is at stake is "a bit of both" or a straightforward dialectic but that precisely what needs closer attention is the range of ways in which opposing imperatives – such as ideologies of frugality and consumption – are related to one another, and how the apparent tension between them can be used as a resource by advertisers, in various ways. This orientation to the greater complexity of such relationships, of course, does not need to be restricted to this historical or geographical context, and the social sciences would do well to give other such opposing imperatives or ideologies similar treatment – exploring the ways that contrary pressures are related to one another in practice rather than tending to focus upon prevalence and diachronic change. Having a closer, more detailed look at specific instances does not afford easy possibilities for grand conclusions, but leads to a less one-dimensional and more nuanced appreciation of empirical material.

Acknowledgements

The author would like to thank John Richardson for his comments on earlier versions of the paper, as well as everyone on the Leverhulme-funded "Changing Families, Changing Food" Programme (award number F/00118/AQ) at the University of Sheffield.

Notes

1. The earliest two advertisements (*WO* 7 December 1945, 17; WO 22 September 1949, 28) are omitted due to space restrictions.
2. The seventh advert stresses Stork's "back again" status.

References

Adkins Covert, T. 2003. Consumption and citizenship during the Second World War: Product advertising in women's magazines. *Journal of Consumer Culture* 3, no. 3: 315–42.

Amouzadeh, M., and M. Tavangar. 2004. Decoding pictorial metaphor: Ideologies in Persian commercial advertising. *International Journal of Cultural Studies* 7, no. 2: 147–74.

Ballaster, R., M. Beetham, E. Frazer, and S. Hebron. 1991. *Women's worlds: Ideology, femininity and the woman's magazine.* Basingstoke: MacMillan.

Bentley, A. 1998. *Eating for victory: Food rationing and the politics of domesticity.* Chicago: University of Illinois Press.

Billig, M., S. Condor, D. Edwards, M. Gane, D. Middleton, and A. Radley. 1988. *Ideological dilemmas: A social psychology of everyday thinking.* London: Sage.

Cook, G. 2001. *The discourse of advertising.* London: Routledge.

Dyer, G. 1982. *Advertising as communication.* London: Routledge.

Machin, D. 2007. *Introduction to multi-modal analysis.* London: Hodder Arnold.

Margarine and Spread Association. 2007. The history of margarine. www.margarine.org.uk/pg_his2.htm (accessed 18 June 2007).

Parkin, K. 2006. *Food is love: Advertising and gender roles in modern America.* Philadelphia: University of Philadelphia Press.

Stork Margarine Cookery Service. 1995. *The art of home cooking.* Crawley: Van Den Berghs.

Waller, J., and M. Vaughan-Rees. 1987. *Women in wartime: The role of women's magazines 1939–1945.* London: Macdonald.

White, C. 1970. *Women's magazines 1693–1968.* London: Michael Joseph.

Williamson, J. 1978. *Decoding advertisements: Ideology and meaning in advertising.* London: Marion Boyars.

Winship, J. 1987. *Inside woman's magazines.* London: Pandora.

Witkowski, TH. 2003. World War II poster campaigns: Preaching frugality to American consumers. *Journal of Advertising* 32, no. 1: 69–82.

Zweiniger-Bargielowska, I. 2000. *Austerity in Britain: Rationing, controls and consumption, 1939–1955.* Oxford: Oxford University Press.

Index

INDEX

INDEX

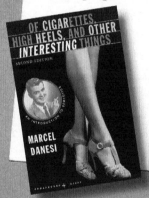

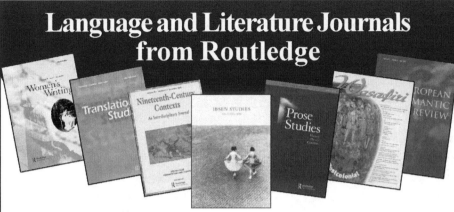